the seafo

FIRST PUBLISHED IN APRIL 2009

BY ESTRAGON PRESS

DURRUS

COUNTY CORK

© ESTRAGON PRESS

TEXT AND RECIPES © MARTIN SHANAHAN & SALLY McKENNA

THE MORAL RIGHT OF THE AUTHORS HAS BEEN ASSERTED

ISBN - 978-1-874076-94-0

TYPESET IN BODONI, GILL SANS & HELVETICA NEUE

PRINTED IN SPAIN BY GRAPHYCEMS

PUBLISHING EDITOR   John McKenna

EDITOR   Judith Casey

PHOTOGRAPHIC CONSULTANT   Kevin O'Farrell

PRODUCTION ASSISTANT   Eve Clancy

WEB   fluidedge

The IASC Skillnet is funded by member companies and the Training Networks Programme, an initiative of Skillnets Ltd. funded from the National Training Fund through the Department of Enterprise, Trade and Employment.

the seafood lover's
cookbook

martin shanahan & sally mckenna

For Marie, Jack,
Ben and Lucy
MS

For Declan, Deirdre
and Packy
SMcK

thanks

Martin Shanahan would like to thank the staff and customers at Fishy Fishy, and to thank our fishermen, whose bravery means that we can enjoy this wonderful gift that is seafood.

Sally McKenna would like to thank Martina and Michelle at IASC, and all at Gill & Macmillan including Alfie, Chris, John, Paul, Karen and Sandra. And, as always, thanks to Connie, Sam and PJ.

A special thanks to all the wonderful IASC members who helped with suggestions, ideas and information, and to those who submitted precious photographs.

photography

Heir Island punt, page 33, Galway hooker, page 47, Whiddy Island pier, page 82, Whiddy Island fishermen, pages 88, 109, 114 and 125, Heir Island Lobster boat, page 109 all by **Kevin O'Farrell**.

Three Portmagee boats, page 83, Mick, Tony & Joe Doyle from Dun Laoghaire, page 134, Fish Auction, page 135, Bun Beag and Bun Brosna, Arklow, page 139 all by kind permission of *The Irish Skipper*. **www.irishskipper.net**

Frank Downey mending nets, page 132, Splitting and curing mackerel, page 144, Castletownbere fishermen mending nets, page 159 all by kind permission of **Mná na Mara**.

Killybegs boat, page 29, and Irish trawler page 157, all by kind permission of **Matty Smith.**

Photo of Kish Fish, page 154, cover photo of Vera Herffernan and filleting image by kind permission of **BIM**.

Fisherman, page 122 by Nick Hoffman.

Directory photos by kind permission of **IASC retailers**.

All other photos by **Sally McKenna**. Food styling by **Martin Shanahan.**

Martin Shanahan

is chef-proprietor, with his wife Marie, of Fishy Fishy Café and Shop in Kinsale. Fishy Fishy is internationally recognised as Ireland's leading seafood restaurant. When not at the stoves, Martin spends much of his time horseriding and sailing. www.fishyfishy.ie

Sally McKenna

Sally McKenna is publisher, with her husband John, of the *Bridgestone Guides*. The *Bridgestone Guides* are regarded by critics and commentators as Ireland's leading food guides. When not at the computer, Sally tries to grab time to go sea kayaking and sailing. www.bridgestoneguides.com

introduction

Heritage and hunting. Health and wealth. A blessing and a bounty.

The people in Ireland who catch and sell fish maintain one of the proudest heritages in our country. Read through the directory of this book and you will meet fishmongers whose grandfathers started off with little boats, and who then started selling fish from carts, and you will meet people who have been handed a vital bloodline that respects and understands the sea and its delicious rewards. Generation after generation. Talk to fishmongers and fishermen and they will say: "It's in the blood".

This bloodline is primordial, for the heritage maintains one of the most extraordinary things about fish: as Howth fishmonger Martin McLoughlin says: "Fish is one of the last things that man has gone out to hunt". Yes there is an increasing amount of farmed fish on the slab, but most of what we cook is wild fish, brought back by people who voyage in hope, and expectation. The voyages are often dangerous, if not fatal, and we hope *The Seafood Lover's Cookbook* shows the respect we feel for the bravery of these sea hunters.

The wealth of the seas is also a vital aspect of our health. Our bodies cannot make the omega-3s that eating fish gives us, and we know now that Mother's old saw: "Eat up your fish, it's brain food!", is totally and absolutely true. We must protect this wealth, and we need concerted political will to do so, for this wealth is, indisputably, nothing less than our future health.

The gift of the seas is a blessing, and it is twice blessed. As these recipes show, the pleasure of cooking fish is outdone only by the pleasure of eating this diverse and utterly delicious bounty.

Cooking and eating fresh fish connects us to a proud Irish heritage. Let's respect and enjoy it.

introduction

contents

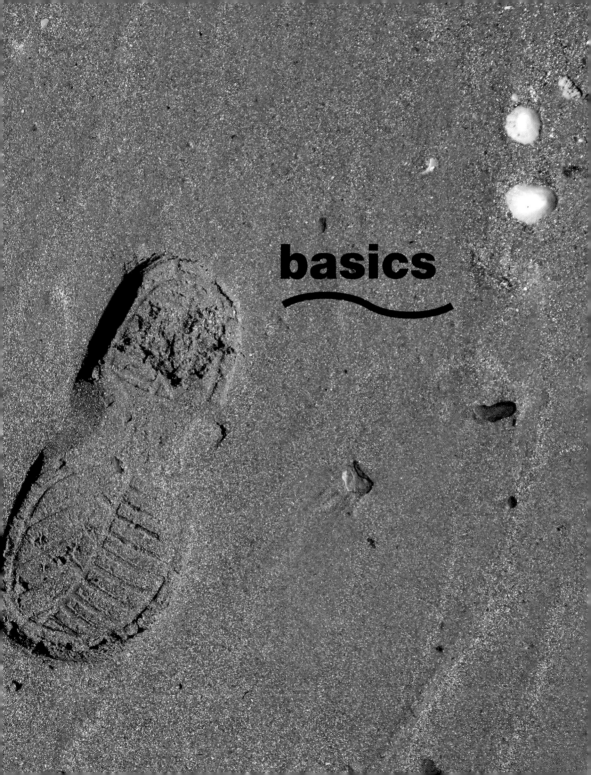

basics

These two everyday recipes are easy to make. The brown bread takes mere seconds, and makes the classic Irish brown loaf, perfect for all seafood dishes.

The recipe for the white loaves uses a mixer with a dough hook. You can also knead it by hand.

Brown Soda Bread

butter or oil to grease 900g loaf tin
450g wholewheat flour
1 tablespoon wheatgerm
1 tablespoon bran
pinch of salt
½ tablespoon bread soda
600ml buttermilk

Preheat the oven to 175°C. Grease or butter a 900g loaf tin. Measure the flour into the bowl, and add the wheatgerm, bran, and salt. Sift in the bread soda. Finally stir in the buttermilk, mixing with a wooden spoon until everything is combined. Place in a greased loaf tin. The dough should reach almost to the top of the tin. Bake in the preheated oven for 50 minutes.

Take out of the oven and let rest on a wire rack until cool. This bread is best served on the day it is made.

Bread

White Yeasted Loaf

1kg strong white bread flour
1 teaspoon salt
1 tablespoon dried yeast
700ml water
1 tablespoon olive oil
olive oil for rubbing the bowl

Place the flour and salt in the bowl of your food mixer and fit with the dough hook. If you are using the instant yeast that is designed to be added straight to flour, add it to the flour now. If you are using dried yeast that is meant to be added to liquid, then add it to the warmed 700ml water, stir, and leave for 10 minutes.

Add the water and olive oil to the flour, switch on your mixer and knead for 10 minutes. Rub a large bowl with olive oil and place the dough inside it. Leave to rise for approximately one and a half hours.

When well risen, punch down the dough and cut in two with a knife. Place in two well-oiled loaf tins and bake in an oven, that has been preheated to 200°C, for approximately 50 minutes.

basics

Stocks and Bouillon

fish bouillon

500ml water
½ cup white wine vinegar
2 bay leaves
salt and 10 cracked peppercorns
the juice of 1 lemon
fresh parsley

Place all the ingredients in a large saucepan, and bring to the boil. Simmer for 10 minutes to infuse the flavours. Strain.

fish stock

heads and bones of 1½kg flat fish
1 carrot, scrubbed and chopped roughly
1 onion, peeled and halved
1 stalk celery, chopped
2 bay leaves
10 crushed black peppercorns
3 litres water

Put all the ingredients into a large saucepan, and bring to the boil. Skim the surface of the foam that will gather, and then simmer for absolutely no more than 15 minutes. Strain.

mushroom stock

fish stock ingredients plus
a handful chopped mushrooms
2 whole cloves garlic
a piece of fresh ginger, roughly chopped

Put all the ingredients into a large saucepan, and bring to the boil. Skim the surface of the foam that will gather, and then simmer for absolutely no more than 15 minutes. Strain.

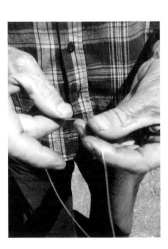

techniques

preparing fresh crab

- Place a large saucepan on the heat and add about 3mm water. Warm the water. Put in the crab, and begin to turn up the heat. (Some people say this is easier for the crab, as it falls asleep. You may prefer to plunge the crab into boiling water, and get the process over more quickly.) Boil the crab for 15 to 20 minutes. Remove and cool completely - for at least 1 hour.

- Turn the cold crab over, remove the legs by pulling in the opposite direction from which they lie. Remove tail flap and discard.

- Next prise open the section, called the purse, to which all the legs were attached. An oyster knife is a good implement to do this with. Throw away this purse.

- Press down the eye section of the crab, and pull away, lifting out the eyes and the stomach sac behind it.

- The shell contains the brown meat and the roe; spoon this out. The brown meat from inside the shell can then be processed in a food processor, after which it forms an absolutely delicious pâté-type mixture.

- To remove the white meat, smash the large front claws of the crab carefully, so as not to smash the meat. Pull away the flesh of the crab, including the meat that you will find in the pincers. The smaller legs don't have much meat in, and are best used as a garnish.

techniques

opening an oyster

- You will need an oyster knife and a cloth. Hold the oyster in the stiff cloth (to protect your hands) with the flatter shell uppermost.

- Find a gap between the upper and lower shell. Slide the knife blade parallel to the upper shell and sever the muscle attached to the oyster.

- Being careful not to lose any of the juices, force the top shell up to open the oyster. Remove the top shell.

- Using the blade of the knife, separate the oyster from the lower shell. Tip out the juices into a jug (you might have to sieve them). Scrape away any fragments of shell from the oyster meat, which is now ready to serve or cook.

shelling fresh prawns

- You can simply split the cooked prawn in half lengthways for an attractive presentation.

- If you want to remove the prawn tail, first twist off the head. Squeeze the prawn tail inwards gently, to break the skin, then carefully peel away the skin to reveal the meaty tail in one piece.

- If it has not already come loose, extract the black vein that runs along the back of the tail, using the tip of a knife.

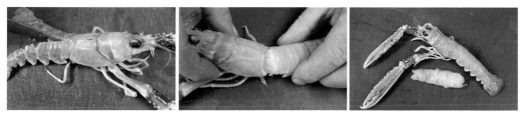

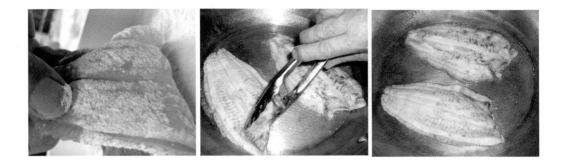

pan-fried fish

- Put a dry frying pan onto the heat, and leave it to heat up.
- Dry the fish, and then dip into seasoned flour, shaking off any excess.
- Pour some oil into the pan, and place the fish, presentation side down. (You might wish to serve the fish with a crispy skin, facing up, or you might have skinned your fish beforehand or you might have a fillet skin side down. Whichever you choose, cook the side you want to see facing you on the plate first.)
- Cook for a couple of minutes, keeping the heat very high, with timing depending on the thickness of your fish.
- Turn the fish over, and cook on the other side. The fish is cooked when it is firm to the touch and a milky, almost translucent, white in colour. Finish with a knob of butter.

roasting fish

- Preheat your oven to at least 200°C.
- Put your frying pan on the hob, over a high heat. You will need a frying pan that can also be put in the oven. (Otherwise you can use a hob-proof baking dish, such as a Le Creuset dish.)
- When the pan is very hot, place some oil in the pan (olive oil is always a good choice, but not extra virgin olive oil).
- Place your fish, presentation side up, into the hot pan. Cook for a couple of minutes, and then lift the whole pan off the stove and place into the oven for a further 5-10 minutes, depending on the thickness of the fish. The fish is cooked when it is firm to the touch and a milky, almost translucent, white in colour.

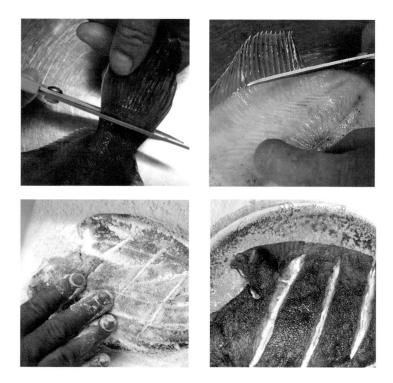

skinning flat fish

● To skin a flat fish, start at the tip of the tail, score into the tail with a sharp knife and loosen a flap of skin. Pull hard on this skin, holding the fish in the other hand. The skin should peel off.
To finish, cut away any remaining bits of skin, and, using a sharp pair of scissors, cut around the edge of the fish.

techniques

skinning fish fillets

• To skin a fish fillet, lay the fillet on a board and, holding the tail skin with one hand, slide a sharp knife between the skin and the fillet. Use a slight sawing action, trying not to cut through either the flesh or the skin. Separate the skin from the fillet. Finally check for any bits of skin, or pin bones, which you can remove with tweezers.

steamed or poached fish or shellfish

• If you have a fish poacher, then this is especially suitable for large fish, otherwise small fish, as well as fish steaks and fillets of fish, can be steamed in any steamer that will accommodate them.

• For steaming fish, use salted water, and for poaching fish, use a bouillon. Poached fish should be simmered, never boiled, while shellfish can be cooked at a gentle boil.

fishy fishy favourites

Sauces and Dressings

Tomato Salsa

2 ripe tomatoes
1 shallot
1 handful leaf coriander
juice of ½ a lime
1 teaspoon sweet chilli sauce
pinch salt

Slice the tomatoes in half, horizontally and remove seeds. Finely dice the flesh of the tomato. Dice the shallot and shred the coriander. Place all the ingredients in a bowl and stir gently to combine. Place in the fridge for 30 minutes before serving.

Roast Red Pepper Salsa

3 red peppers
1 dessertspoon capers
juice of 1 lime
1 chilli, finely sliced
coriander

Preheat the oven to 200°C. Cut the peppers in half and brush with olive oil. Roast cut side down for 15-20 minutes. Place in a bowl covered with cling film. Leave for 10 minutes, then peel and cut into fine slices. Mix together all the ingredients.

fishy fishy favourites

Rocket Oil/Parsley Oil

200g rocket or parsley
2 cups olive oil
Blanch the parsley or rocket (including stems) in boiling water for about 10-15 seconds. Refresh in a bowl of iced water. Drain and dry in a salad spinner. Blend 1 cup of oil with the herbs in a blender. Add the second cup of oil. Pour through a paper coffee filter into a jug and then bottle. Stored in the fridge this oil will keep well for a week.

Lemon Butter Sauce

275ml cream
80g butter
juice of 1 lemon
salt and white pepper
Place all the ingredients in a small saucepan and bring to the boil. Cook over a moderately high heat until it reduces to a thick sauce.

Asian Butter Sauce

125g butter
2 tablespoons sweet chilli sauce
2½cm fresh ginger, cut into julienned slivers
2 spring onions, shredded
1 bunch coriander, roughly chopped
Melt the butter and add the rest of the ingredients. Keep warm, stir and use as a sauce.

6

Flavours for Mayonnaise

• **Rocket Mayonnaise:** Place 1 cup mayonnaise, 60g rocket and the juice of ½ lemon in a food processor and whiz until blended.

• **Lime and Lemon Mayonnaise:** Mix together 300ml mayonnaise, juice of 1 lemon, juice of 2 limes.

• **Cocktail Sauce:** Mix together 1 cup mayonnaise, ¼ cup tomato ketchup, 1 tablespoon Worcester sauce, 1 teaspoon Tabasco, 1 tablespoon grated horseradish.

• **Tartare Sauce:** Mix together ½ cup mayonnaise, 2 anchovies, 1 tablespoon capers, chopped, 4 gherkins, chopped, generous handful fresh parsley, chopped.

• **Curry Aïoli** Mix together 1 cup mayonnaise, 1 teaspoon lemon juice, 1 tablespoon curry paste, 1 clove garlic, finely minced.

• **Tarragon and orange mayonnaise** Mix together 1 cup mayonnaise, 1 tablespoon tarragon vinegar, grated zest of 1 orange, juice of ½ an orange, salt and pepper, 1 tablespoon finely chopped fresh tarragon.

Roast Red Pepper Dressing

2 red peppers
olive oil
300ml mayonnaise
150ml white wine vinegar
30g sugar
1 clove garlic, minced
salt and pepper

Preheat the oven to maximum. Cut the peppers in half and remove their seeds. Brush the skin with olive oil. Place on a hot tray in the preheated oven and roast until the skin blackens (about 10-15 minutes). Take out of the oven and place in a bowl, and cover with cling film.

Cool for 10 minutes, and then skin the peppers. Place with all the rest of the ingredients into a blender and blend until smooth. Season to taste.

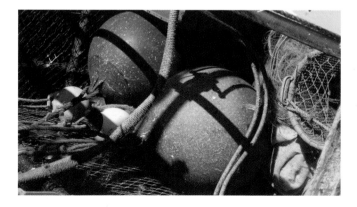

Mango and Green Peppercorn Dressing

juice of ½ a lime
1 tablespoon white wine vinegar
1 teaspoon freshly grated ginger
½ teaspoon salt
½ cup olive oil
1 tablespoon boiling water
1 teaspoon green peppercorns
½ cup diced mango (or to taste)

Place all the ingredients (except the mango) in a small bowl and whisk together. Then stir in the mango.

fishy fishy favourites

Sides and Garnishes

Potato Boxty

3 large potatoes (approximately 550g)
1 teaspoon salt and freshly ground pepper
50g butter, melted
oil for frying the boxty

Grate the potatoes and put in a clean tea-towel. Squeeze out as much moisture as you can. Place the potatoes in a bowl and season with salt and pepper and pour over the melted butter. Stir well.

Heat a generous quantity of oil in a frying pan and place serving spoonfuls of the mixture onto the hot pan. Try to keep the spoonfuls the same size. Cook over a fairly high heat, turning after approximately five minutes. The outside of the boxty should be crispy, the inside just cooked.

Parsnip Chips

1 fresh parsnip
oil for deep-fat frying

Peel the parsnip, then slice into very thin slices, using a potato peeler. Deep fry for 1 minute in a deep-fat fryer, heated to 190°C.

fishy fishy favourites

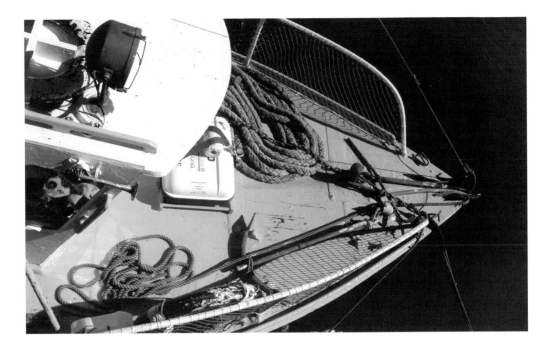

Avocado Cream

2 Haas avocados
the juice of ½ a lemon
¼ cup crème fraîche
1 red chilli, finely sliced or 2 tablespoons chilli sauce
salt and pepper
¼ cup single cream

Blend the avocados, lemon juice, and crème fraîche in a blender until you get a smooth purée. Add the sliced chilli and season. If you want to, you can use this now, as a mild guacamole dip. If you want to use it as a cream, then at this point add the ¼ cup of single cream. Use a squeezy bottle, or empty ketchup bottle, to drizzle this over your dish.

fishy fishy favourites

Chickpea Fritters

You can make these fritters in advance. Pre-cook them for 2-3 minutes, then, when you are ready to use them place on a baking sheet and warm for 10 minutes in an 190°C preheated oven.

250g dried chickpeas
1 onion
3 cloves garlic
¼ cup finely chopped parsley
1 tablespoon ground cumin
1 tablespoon ground coriander
1 teaspoon baking powder
6 tablespoons water
1 teaspoon salt
black pepper
1 teaspoon curry powder
oil for deep frying

Soak the chickpeas in water overnight. Drain, and then place in a food processor - you will probably have to do this in batches. Process until you have ground the chickpeas very finely. Finely chop the onion, and mince the garlic. Mix all the ingredients and leave to rest for half an hour.

When ready to cook, take lumps of the mixture, the size of a golf ball. Roll up and flatten slightly, and let rest for a further 15 minutes on a plate. Heat the oil in the deep-fat fryer to 170°C, and deep fry the fritters for about 3-4 minutes until golden brown.

fishy fishy favourites

Pickled Red Onion

2 red onions
¼ cup white wine vinegar
¼ cup caster sugar
pinch salt

Peel the onions then slice into fine rings. Separate the rings to make small, thin circles of onion. In a small bowl, mix the vinegar and the sugar together with a fork, until the sugar is dissolved, then add the salt. Marinate the onion rings in this vinegar for an hour.

Fresh Herb Salad

A small bowlful of herbs, including coriander, chervil, flat leaf parsley and chives
2 spring onions
1 red chilli
the juice of ½ lemon
2 tablespoons olive oil
salt and pepper

Wash the herbs and remove the stalks from all except the coriander, then tear them into pieces. Slice the spring onions and red chilli into very thin strips, or julienne. In a bowl, mix together the lemon juice and olive oil and season with a little salt and pepper. Toss the vegetables and herbs in this mixture just before serving.

Roasted Fennel

2 fennel bulbs
olive oil
salt and pepper
½ cup chicken stock

Preheat the oven to 190°C. Cut the fennel bulbs in quarters, making sure to leave a little of the heart attached - this will keep the quarters together. Put a heavy, oven-proof pan on the heat for about 6 minutes until fiercely hot. Brush the fennel with olive oil and place the quarters in the hot pan, searing the two cut sides. Transfer the pan to the oven. Sprinkle over pepper and salt, and pour over the chicken stock. Cook for about 20 minutes until the stock evaporates and the fennel softens.

fishy fishy favourites

Chickpea, Orange & Chive Salad

250g dried chickpeas

dressing:
2 tablespoons white wine vinegar
75mls olive oil
2 oranges
large handful of chives
1 tablespoon pickled pink peppercorns

Soak the chickpeas over night. Drain and cook for 40 minutes in boiling water into which you have placed some aromatics for flavouring (half and onion, a stick of celery, black pappercorns, a carrot).

Cut the orange into segments: slice the top and bottom of the orange off with a sharp knife, then, moving the knife towards you peel off thick slices from the orange taking both the skin and the white pith away from the orange. Working over a bowl, cut into the segments. Squeeze what remains of the orange extracting the juice. Whisk together the vinegar, olive oil and extracted orange juice and stir in the chives and pink peppercorns.

Toss the chickpeas and orange segments in this dressing.

Roast Winter Vegetables

a mixture of the following:
celeriac
parsnip
turnip
red onion
whole garlic
olive oil
thyme leaves
parsley
salt and pepper

Peel the vegetables and cut the root vegetables into batons, the onions into quarters and leave the garlic whole.

Heat some olive oil in an ovenproof pan and pan fry all the vegetables with the whole garlic and thyme leaves. Cook like this for a couple of minutes to colour the vegetables. Transfer the whole pan into the oven, season with salt and pepper and roast at 200°C for 15-20 minutes, or until cooked through. Sprinkle over some parsley and serve hot.

soups

Kinsale Gourmet Chowder

Most fishmongers make up a chowder mix - a good mix for this would include cod, whiting, salmon, ling, white pollock and haddock. This mix should not include a smoked fish.

You can garnish this soup with a tablespoon of fresh crab or a fresh shrimp and some lightly whipped cream.

400g prawn heads
1 tablespoon cooking oil
200g carrots, scrubbed and chopped
200g onions, peeled and chopped
½ cup tomato purée
2 litres fish stock
2 cloves garlic
1 tablespoon olive oil
1 tablespoon dried French tarragon
1 tablespoon ground coriander
375g mixture of fish, diced
170ml carton cream
50g butter
50g flour

Preheat your oven to 220°C and roast the prawn heads on a baking tray, sprinkled with the cooking oil for 10 minutes. Then place in a large saucepan with the carrots, onions, tomato purée and 2 litres stock. Simmer for 1 hour. Strain. In another saucepan, sauté the garlic and herbs in the olive oil, add the diced fish, and when just cooked add the cream and remove from the heat. Make a paste with 50g soft butter and 50g flour. Spoon a little of the hot prawn stock into the paste, stirring to thin it slightly. Pour this thinned paste back into the hot prawn stock, stirring over the heat at the same time, and continue stirring until you get a thickened stock. Turn down the heat and add the creamed fish mixture. Let the two mixtures infuse, then serve.

Rouille

Rouille is the ultimate garnish for a seafood soup.

sea salt
1 tablespoon dried red chilli flakes
1 clove garlic
10 peppercorns
1 slice day old white bread, crust removed
3 red peppers, grilled, peeled and chopped
1 cup extra virgin olive oil

Using a mortar and pestle, pound the salt, chilli flakes, garlic and peppercorns to a paste. Soak the bread in warm water and then squeeze dry. Pound this with the chilli mixture. Next, add the red peppers and pound again. Finally, add the olive oil, drop by drop as if you were making mayonnaise. (You might have to remove a little of the mixture if your pestle is not big enough. Simply stir the portion you removed back into the mix after you have added the oil.) You should finish with a thick sauce consistency.

Seafood Soup

with Pasta and Rouille

Don't be shy to ask your fishmonger for heads and carcasses to use in stock or to make this soup - though they might appreciate some advance notice.

The bones of flat fish are best for making any stock or soup.

2 tablespoons olive oil
2 onions, roughly chopped
salt
1 can tomatoes
4 garlic cloves, left whole and unpeeled
2 bay leaves
the zest of ½ an orange
1 bunch fennel leaves
splash of Pernod
heads and carcasses of three large flat fish
tagliatelle or pappardelle pasta
rouille (see left)

Heat the oil in a large saucepan and add the onions and salt. Cook until soft. Add the tomatoes, whole garlic, bayleaves, zest and the fennel plus a splash of Pernod. Wash out the can of tomatoes with fresh water and add the water to the mixture. Simmer for about half an hour.

Add the fish bones and add boiling water to cover. Simmer for another 20 minutes (and no more). Take off the heat and pour the soup into another pan, through a fine sieve. Use a pestle or wooden spoon to squeeze out as much as you can through the sieve then discard the fish mixture. Reheat the soup. Cook the pasta separately in some salted boiling water, strain and add to the hot soup. Serve with rouille.

Potato and Leek Seafood Soup

Fresh seafood added to any vegetable soup can give it a whole new dimension.

For this recipe you could use whiting, haddock, ling or white pollock.

2 litres fish stock or water
salt and pepper
500g potatoes
500g leeks
3 fillets firm round fish, skinned and diced
butter

Bring the stock or water to the boil and season. Peel and slice the potatoes, wash and slice the leeks and add to the boiling water or stock.

Skim as the soup heats up, and then simmer for 30 minutes, until the potatoes are just breaking apart.

Add the sliced pieces of fish. Cook for five minutes more and then serve with a knob of butter in each bowl.

soups

A Bowl of Mussels

Every year Martin and his family spend summer holidays in a mobile home at the seaside - here a big bowl of mussels, served straight from the saucepan with crusty bread, is their regular summer feast.

If you have time, it's a good idea to put the mussels in a large bowl of fresh water, into which you have sprinkled a handful of oatmeal. The mussels take in the fresh water while eating the oatmeal, and it helps to get rid of any grit or impurities.

Cleaning and Cooking Mussels

- Tip mussels into a bowl and shake fairly aggressively until they all close (discard any that don't close). Rinse under fresh cold water. Drain. Put a large saucepan on the stove to heat and tip in the mussels. Cover and leave for a few minutes until the mussels open (discard any that don't open).

Bowl of Mussels with Curry Aïoli

See page 26 for recipe for curry aïoli. Serve with chips - dip the mussels and chips alternately into the aïoli.

Mussels in Butter Sauce

Add a glass of white wine or cider when cooking the mussels, along with two diced shallots, a handful of chopped parsley and a large knob of butter. When the mussels have opened, transfer them to a heated serving bowl. Strain the cooking liquid and boil it to reduce until thickened. Add another large chunk of butter, the juice of a lemon and some more parsley. Pour over the mussels and serve.

Belgian Steamcd Mussels

Sauté some shallots and celery in a large knob of butter until soft. Add the mussels, some fresh thyme and bay leaf, some parsley and a generous amount of black pepper. Pour over a glass of white wine and cook on high heat until the mussels open. Serve the lot in deep bowls. Chips essential.

Wok Fried Mussels

Put the mussels into a wok with a little drop of water. Put on the heat and cook until the mussels open. Drain the water (you can reserve the juice for a stock or sauce). Add some Asian butter (see page 25) and serve garnished with some toasted sesame seeds.

fishy treats

Squid with Chorizo

~~~~~~~~

Scoring the squid before cooking helps the fish to cook more evenly. It is essential to do this if you're using large squid.

Squid is available all year, but the quality and availability is best from October to March.

1 cup aged balsamic vinegar (3-5 year old)
¼ cup sugar
300g squid
1 fresh chorizo
wild rocket

Put the balsamic vinegar and sugar in a small saucepan and boil until it has reduced by half. Cut the squid lengthways and score the inside of the squid with a sharp knife, cutting a little way through the surface, but not right through. Then dice the squid into pieces about 2½ cm square. Pan fry the squid over a high heat along with the diced chorizo. Cook for about a minute before putting on the plate and topping with some wild rocket. Drizzle over some of the reduced vinegar. These quantities make enough for about two servings.

Shellfish Crumble

All of these ingredients can be prepared ahead and just put together at the last minute.

Crab, prawn and shrimps can be bought most of the year, but the best availability and quality is during the months April to September.

This is the ultimate seaside holiday dish, made in the summer when the fish is at its best.

100g breadcrumbs
3 cloves garlic
2 tablespoons finely chopped parsley
double portion of Lemon Butter Sauce
200g white crab meat
150g fresh prawns
150g shrimps

Mix the breadcrumbs with the very finely chopped garlic and the parsley.

Make up a double portion of Lemon Butter Sauce (see page 25 for recipe). This will make a little more than you need, but Lemon Butter Sauce has a thousand other uses, so don't fret. When you are nearly ready to serve the crumble, divide the fish between four to six single serving oven-proof dishes. Pour some sauce over each one and scatter liberally with the breadcrumb mixture.

Cook the crumbles in an oven pre-heated to 200°C for around 10 minutes, or until the bread-crumbs are crispy (watch - they burn easily) and the mixture is hot right through.

Potted Smoked and Fresh Salmon

225g poached salmon, skinned
175g smoked salmon, skinned
3 tablespoons crème fraíche
1 tablespoon creamed horseradish
1 tablespoon chopped dill
1 tablespoon chopped chives
pinch cayenne pepper
juice of half a lemon
salt and pepper
100g butter

Flake the poached salmon and cut the smoked salmon into very fine dice. Mix the fish together along with the crème fraíche, horseradish, dill, chives, cayenne pepper, and lemon juice. Taste and season with salt and pepper.

Heat the butter until just melted and then fold most of it into the fish mixture, reserving a little for the tops.

Divide between six little ramekins, top with the reserved melted butter and chill for at least an hour in the fridge before serving.

Smoked Mackerel Pâté

250g smoked mackerel
25g butter plus a little for topping
1 tablespoon chopped dill
1 tablespoon chopped chives
juice of 1 lemon
salt and pepper
1 tablespoon grated horseradish
¼ cup/80ml pouring cream
pinch of paprika

Flake the fish, dice the butter and put all the ingredients into a food processor. Pulse for about a minute until the pâté comes together. Spoon into four small ramekin dishes and top with melted butter. Chill in the fridge for at least an hour before serving with toast.

Fishy Fishy Crab Cocktail

1 recipe tomato salsa (see page 25)
shredded lettuce
375g white crab meat
120ml cocktail sauce (see page 26)
crab claws (for decoration)
brown crab meat (optional)

In Fishy Fishy Café this crab cocktail is served in tall glasses. Take four of these glasses and fill the base with the tomato salsa. Next, put a layer of shredded lettuce on top of the salsa. Then top with the white crab meat. Drizzle over some cocktail sauce and garnish with a crab claw and a little more lettuce.

If you have brown crab meat, you can serve this in a small ramekin, alongside.

Crab Claws
in Lemon Butter Sauce

500g crab claws
275ml lemon butter sauce (see page 25)
parsley oil (see page 25)
sweet chilli sauce

Toss the crab claws in the lemon butter sauce. Drizzle over some parsley oil and sweet chilli sauce.

Hot Oysters in their Shell

with Horseradish

12 oysters
juice of ½ lemon
¼ cup cream
1 tablespoon horseradish cream

Open the oysters and remove from their shells, reserving the juice. Put the oyster and lemon-juice, horseradish and cream into a small pan, heat and poach the oysters in their juice for about a minute. Spoon the mixture back into the oysters.

Seaweed makes an attractive garnish for oysters, both cooked and raw. Gather the seaweed from the beach, bring home and plunge into boiling water for about 30 seconds until it turns bright green. Refresh in cold water and drain.

Note this is not an edible garnish!

fishy treats

Vinegar Mackerel

Serve this mackerel cold on cocktail sticks with some of the cooking liquor, some sliced tomatoes and sliced red onion – the ultimate Irish tapas.

4 whole mackerel, cleaned
1 carrot, sliced
1 bay leaf
1 sprig parsley
1 sprig thyme
8 peppercorns
350ml white wine vinegar

Preheat the oven to its highest setting. Place the mackerel in an ovenproof casserole with a tight-fitting lid. Add the other ingredients and add water to cover. Bake for 15-20 minutes in the oven until the liquid gets just hot enough to cook the fish. Take the mackerel from the mixture, saving the liquid. Scrape away the skin and lift the fillets away from the bone. Cut into slices and place in a bowl. Strain over some cooking liquor. Chill.

fish for breakfast

Soufflé Omelette

with smoked salmon, spinach and fresh crab

4 slices smoked salmon
chives
6 eggs
½ cup crab meat
½ cup cooked spinach
salt and pepper
100g butter

Slice the salmon into slivers. Snip the chives with scissors. Separate the yolks from the whites of the eggs. Beat the yolks with a fork and add the salmon, crab, spinach and chives and pepper. Don't over mix.

Beat the whites with the salt until they form stiff peaks, then add to the yolks. Stir to just combine, but no more. Heat an omelette pan. Add the butter and then the eggs. Put the lid on and turn down the heat. Cook for approximately 2 minutes then serve with hot toast.

Lemon Sole
pan-fried with parsley butter

~~~

You could substitute plaice or John Dory for the lemon sole.

2 tablespoons finely chopped parsley
25g butter
zest of ½ a lemon
squeeze of lemon juice
salt
2 fillets of lemon sole
seasoned flour
extra butter for frying

Mix together the parsley, butter, lemon zest, lemon juice and salt. The best way to do this is to use a pestle and mortar. Dry the fish with kitchen paper and dust with seasoned flour. Pan fry the fillets in the butter and then put one on each plate.

Place a generous teaspoon of parsley butter on each fillet (you can either spread this out on the fish, or leave in a dollop in the centre).

Smoked Haddock

with Scrambled Eggs and Toast

450g fillet of smoked haddock
milk
6 eggs
butter
pepper

Place the haddock in a shallow pan. Cover with milk and heat gently until the fish is hot. Keep warm in the milk while you make the scrambled eggs.

Lightly whip the eggs with a fork. Melt some butter in a frying pan and add the eggs. Season with pepper. Cook gently over a low heat, stirring regularly until the eggs are scrambled.

Divide the eggs between four plates, and serve with some lightly poached haddock and hot buttered toast.

Oatmeal-fried Mackerel and Bacon

for each person:
salt and freshly ground black pepper
1 tablespoon oatmeal
1 mackerel, filleted
generous knob of butter
2 rashers of smoked bacon
lemon wedge
parsley

Put the salt and pepper and oatmeal onto a plate and press the mackerel fillets down on top. The oatmeal should stick to the fish.

Melt a generous knob of butter in a frying pan and fry the bacon until just crisp. Remove the bacon, and keep warm.

Place the fish, flesh side down in the bacon, buttery juices and cook for approximately 3 minutes. Turn over and cook for a further 3 minutes, or until the mackerel is cooked.

Put the mackerel and bacon on the plate and drizzle over any pan juices that remain.

Serve garnished with a lemon wedge and a sprinkling of parsley. Goes equally well with boiled potatoes or buttered slices of brown soda bread.

fish for lunch

Open Fresh Prawn Sandwiches

You can also make these sandwiches with fresh or smoked salmon.

wholemeal bread
butter
fresh prawns
cocktail sauce
green salad
tomato salsa
pickled red onion
parsnip crisps
capers

Place a mixed salad in the centre of each plate. Butter the brown bread and top with fresh prawns, spoon over some cockail sauce and garnish with a combination of tomato salsa, pickled red onion, parsnip crisps and capers. See our chapters on Fishy Fishy Favourites and Sides for recipes for these garnishes.

Asparagus, Crab and New Potato Salad

with Mustard and Dill Dressing

10ml Dijon mustard
1 tablespoon honey
2 tablespoons white wine vinegar
75ml olive oil
salt and pepper
chopped fresh dill
12 spears of asparagus
knob of butter
pinch of sugar
1 kg potatoes
500g fresh white crab meat

Make the dressing first: place the mustard and honey and vinegar in a blender or food processor. Stream in the oil, blending until you get a thick sauce. Add the chopped dill.

Cook the asparagus in some boiling water with a knob of butter and a pinch of sugar. When cooked slice into thirds.

Steam the potatoes until they are just cooked and then, while still warm, toss in the dressing (reserving a little for presentation).

Arrange the potato salad on a large platter. Tuck in the pieces of asparagus and top with the fresh crab. Drizzle over the reserved dressing.

Butterflied grilled Mackerel

with Peanut Sauce

Ask your fishmonger for butterflied fillets of mackerel – where the two fillets are cut so that they are still joined along the back.

Peanut sauce
1 tablespoon fish sauce
1 tablespoon boiling water
2 chillies, finely diced
juice of 1 lime
2 cloves garlic, grated
1 tablespoon freshly grated ginger
1 tablespoon sugar
100g roasted salted peanuts
1 teaspoon sesame oil
1 teaspoon honey

4 whole mackerel
olive oil for brushing

First make the sauce. Place all the ingredients for the sauce in a food processor and pulse until the sauce just comes together.

Brush the mackerel with oil and grill under a hot grill for about 8 minutes. Serve with the sauce.

fish for lunch

Prawn Spring Rolls

220g lean pork, cut in thin strips

225g prawn tails, cut in thin strips

3 tablespoons vegetable oil

4 cloves garlic, minced

3cm ginger, grated

6 spring onions, cut into thin
   strips

400g carrots, peeled and cut into
thin strips

220g mange tout, trimmed and cut
into thin strips

handful fresh beansprouts

the white of 1 egg

Marinade:

2 teaspoons salt

2 teaspoons sugar

black pepper

2 tablespoons Shaohsing wine

2 teaspoons potato flour

2 teaspoons soy sauce

2 teaspoons sesame oil

1½ tablespoons water

Spring Roll wrappers, about 15

This quantity of ingredients makes a large number of prawn spring rolls – great for a party.

If you've made too many, however, they freeze well.

Spring roll wrappers can be found in good delis and all Asian shops.

Mix together the marinade ingredients and marinade the pork and prawns for 15 minutes. Heat a wok over a high heat and add the vegetable oil. Add the garlic, ginger and spring onion. Toss quickly and then immediately add the pork and prawn mixture. Cook until brown and separate, keeping the heat high. Add the carrots and mange tout and stir fry till wilted. Let the mixture go cold, and then add the beansprouts.
You will need around 15 spring roll wrappers. Take each one and place a dollop of the mixture on one side of the wrapper. Begin to roll up. When you get about half way fold in the sides and continue to roll. When fully rolled, seal the edges with a little egg white. Heat oil in a deep fat fryer to around 180°C. Deep fry each roll until it turns pale golden and floats to the surface. Serve hot. If you need to crisp and reheat then deep fry for a second time for a couple of minutes.

John Dory with Anchovy Rosemary Butter, Avocado and Orange Salad

avocado and orange salad:

2 oranges

2 avocados

juice of ½ a lemon

¼ cup cream

salt and pepper

4 large or 8 small fillets of John Dory

seasoned flour

olive oil

75g butter

8 anchovies

1 teaspoon finely chopped rosemary

zest of ½ a lemon

salt and black pepper

To make the salad: slice off the top and bottom of the orange with a sharp knife, then, moving the knife towards you, peel off thick slices from the orange taking both the skin and the white pith away from the orange. Working over a bowl, cut into the segments. Mix the orange segments with the sliced avocado. Mix together the lemon juice and cream, season and pour over the avocado and orange. Dip the John Dory in seasoned flour and pan-fry in a little of the butter and a splash of oil. Remove and keep warm while you add the rest of the butter to the hot pan, and melt the anchovies into this warm butter. Season and serve drizzled over the fish with the salad separately.

fish for lunch

Thai Fish Cakes

cucumber dipping sauce:
75ml rice wine vinegar
75g caster sugar
1 tablespoon Thai fish sauce
half a cucumber, seeded and finely diced
1 medium-sized carrot, peeled and finely diced
3 spring onions (white parts only), diced
1 red chilli, seeded and diced

400g white fish fillets, skinned
1 egg
2 slices crustless white bread torn into pieces
1 tablespoon Thai red curry paste
1 tablespoon Thai fish sauce
1 clove garlic, chopped
40g French beans, finely chopped
handful fresh coriander, chopped
oil for cooking

To make the dipping sauce: put the rice vinegar and sugar and a tablespoon of water into a small pan. Heat, stirring to dissolve the sugar, then boil for 1 minute. Pour into a bowl and allow to go completely cold. When cold, stir in the fish sauce, followed by the very finely diced cucumber, carrot, onion and chilli.

To make the fish cakes: make sure the fish has no skin or bones, and then either put in a food processor, or preferably in a mincer, along with the egg, bread, curry paste, fish sauce and garlic. Mince or process to a paste.

Place the fish in a bowl and add the finely chopped beans and coriander. Mix well.

To form and cook the fish cakes: wet your hands and make eight cakes from the mixture. Shallow fry the fish cakes in some oil, cooking on both sides until golden and cooked. Served with the dipping sauce.

fish for lunch

Coconut Mussels

with Noodles

~~~~~~~~

4 kg mussels, in their shells
1 litre mild chicken stock
1 tablespoon curry powder
400ml coconut milk
4 spring onions, finely sliced
100g snow peas, julienned
juice of 1 lime

4 portions Asian noodles

Carefully scrub and debeard the mussels, removing any barnacles. Discard any that won't close. Bring the chicken stock to the boil in a large saucepan, and stir in the curry powder. Add the mussels, place the lid on the saucepan, and cook until the mussels have opened. Remove the mussels and strain the stock through a very fine sieve, or a normal sieve lined with a piece of muslin. Take just about all the mussels out of their shells, leaving a few for garnishing each bowl. Put the stock back on the heat, and stir in the coconut milk. When the two liquids are well combined, add the spring onions, the snow peas and the lime juice. Cook the noodles according to the instructions on the packet and place in four bowls. Heat the coconut liquid, return the mussels to the pan and pour over the noodles. Serve in bowls.

fish for lunch

Caesar Salad with Fresh Crab

2 cloves garlic
4 anchovies
2 teaspoons red wine vinegar
juice of ½ a lemon
1 teaspoon Worcester sauce
½ teaspoon mustard powder
125ml olive oil
romaine lettuce
croutons
fresh crab

Crush the garlic and anchovies to a paste using a pestle and mortar or a food processor. Add the vinegar, lemon juice, Worcester sauce and mustard powder. Stir together and then beat in the oil.

To assemble the salad, dress the lettuce with the anchovy dressing. Divide between serving plates. Sprinkle over the croutons and top with fresh crab.

Pasta with Blue Cheese and Smoked Salmon

~~~~~~~~~

This is a useful lunch to serve during the christmas season, when you might well have a bit of smoked salmon and blue cheese in the fridge.

25g butter
75g blue cheese (Cashel Blue works well)
100ml cream
small handful chopped thyme
juice of 1 lemon
100g smoked salmon
2 servings of tagliatelle pasta

Melt the butter in a frying pan and then add the crumbled blue cheese. Stir to melt the cheese, then add the cream and thyme.

Cook the pasta separately while making the sauce.

Just before serving squeeze in the lemon juice and add the salmon to the sauce.

Drain the pasta, divide between two bowls and pour over the blue cheese and salmon sauce.

fish for lunch

Warm Chilli Seafood Salad

Martin can't take this off the menu at the Fishy Fishy Café

a mixture of firm fish (poached salmon, monkfish, scallops and if possible include a cooked whole langoustine)
seasoned flour
olive oil
sweet chilli sauce
coriander
spring onion
salad leaves
roast pepper dressing (see page 28)
potato wedges and parsnip chips to serve

Cut the fish into finger-sized slices. Halve the scallops, but keep the langoustine whole. Dip the fish in seasoned flour and pan fry in hot oil. Add the sweet chilli sauce, coriander and spring onion. Toss the salad leaves in the red pepper dressing. Arrange in a bowl with the warm fish on top. Garnish with potato wedges and parsnip chips.

Fish Cakes
3 ways

Shallow fry these cakes in a little bit of olive oil for approximately 5 minutes each side, until crisp.

• **Skate, black pepper & thyme:** 250g skate, boned, 325g mashed potato, fresh thyme leaves, chopped, crushed black pepper, salt, seasoned flour. Steam the fish until just cooked, allow to cool and then flake into pieces. Mix together with the potato, the thyme and black pepper. Season with salt. Wet your hands and form mixture into fish cakes. Dip into the seasoned flour (dust off the excess) and place in the fridge to rest.

• **Salmon and creamed leek:** 250g organic fresh salmon, 100g leek, sliced, cooked and mixed with a little fresh cream, 325g mashed potato, salt and pepper, seasoned flour. Steam the fish until just cooked, allow to cool and then flake into small pieces. Mix together with the creamed leek and the mashed potato. Season the mixture. Wet your hands, then form into fish cakes – this amount of fish and potato should make six good-sized cakes – then dip into the seasoned flour (dust off the excess). Place in the fridge to rest.

• **Crab, red pepper & celery:** 250g white crab meat, 325g mashed potato, 1 red pepper, seeded and finely diced, 2 stalks of celery, stringed and finely chopped, salt and pepper, seasoned flour, 1 egg, beaten with a fork, breadcrumbs. Mix together the crab, potato and vegetables. Season with salt and pepper. Wet your hands, then form into fish cakes, and dip into the seasoned flour (dust off the excess), then the egg, and finally cover with the breadcrumbs. Place in the fridge to rest.

fish for lunch

Naturally Smoked Haddock Risotto with summer peas and lemon

1 onion, diced
2 tablespoons olive oil
300g arborio risotto rice
1¼ litres chicken stock
1 cup peas (fresh or frozen)
zest of 1 lemon
300g smoked haddock
1 tablespoon crème fraîche
salt and pepper
parsley or chervil

Martin cooked this delightfully simple risotto to highlight the beautiful smoked haddock which he sources from local producer Yawl Bay.

Smoked haddock needs no further cooking - you could slice it and eat it cold like smoked salmon. In this recipe, just warm it through with the risotto at the end of cooking.

Sauté the onion in the olive oil until soft. Add the rice and stir until the rice is coated. Heat the chicken stock in another saucepan, and then add the stock to the rice, one ladleful at a time, stirring until the stock is absorbed between each ladle. When all the stock is absorbed, add the peas and the lemon zest. Skin the haddock, and slice - there's no need to pre-cook it. Fold the fish into the risotto and let the risotto rest for a couple of minutes with the lid on. Finally stir in the crème fraîche. Season and scatter over the parsley or chervil. Serve immediately.

Roast Marinated Sea Trout

with Asian Sauce and Noodle Salad

2 large filets sea trout

marinade:
¼ cup rice vinegar
¼ cup soy sauce
1 tablespoon grated ginger
2 tablespoons hoisin sauce
2 teaspoons Shaohsing wine or sherry

sauce:
¼ cup soy sauce
¼ cup sesame oil
2 teaspoons sugar
sesame seeds

Marinate the fish in the marinade ingredients for 15 minutes. Place the fish in a hot roasting tin and roast for 10 minutes. Mix together the sauce ingredients and drizzle over the cooked trout.

fish for lunch

Noodle Salad

200g noodles
2 teaspoons sesame oil
1 tablespoon groundnut oil
2 tablespoons lime juice
1 teaspoon wasabi
1 teaspoon grated ginger
1 teaspoon fish sauce
2 spring onions, sliced at an angle
1 chilli, finely diced
mixture of any of the following, sliced: green pepper, mange tout, carrot, broccoli

Cook the noodles according to the instructions on the packet. Stir together the sesame oil, ground nut oil, lime juice, wasabi, grated ginger and fish sauce. Toss together with the spring onions and chilli, and a handful of the vegetables.

fish for lunch

seafood
barbecue

Seafood BBQ Ideas

- ## Split Prawns with Garlic
Take about 12 Dublin Bay prawns, heads on, and split them right down the middle (splitting the head in half as well). Mix together 2 tablespoons red wine vinegar, salt and pepper, 1 teaspoon fennel seeds, 1 chilli, finely chopped, 2 cloves garlic, finely chopped. Whisk in 6 tablespoons olive oil. Pour over the prawns to marinate. When ready to eat grill the prawns for a few minutes on the fire.

- ## Scallops in their Shell
Open the scallop shells and clean the scallops. Return the fish to the flat part of the shell, and place the shell on the fire to cook the scallop.

- ## Monkfish tails wrapped in bacon
Wrap whole small monkfish tails in bacon, completely wrapping the fish in the meat. Tie up with cotton string and barbecue.

- ## Mackerel with Chermoula
Make a chermoula dressing by mixing 3 cloves chopped garlic, the peel from some preserved lemon, or the peel of half a lemon, a bunch of flat-leaf parsley and coriander, a couple of bay leaves, some thyme leaves, 1 teaspoon paprika, half teaspoon ground cumin, a pinch of chilli power, the juice of one lemon and 50ml olive oil. Score the whole mackerel and rub some of the chermoula inside each fish. Grill for approximately 5 minutes each side, and serve with the remaining chermoula.

seafood barbecue

• Mussel and Clam bake

Cut a double layer of kitchen foil, large enough to take your mussels and clams. Wash the shellfish, drain and place in the kitchen foil. Roll up carefully to make a bag - making sure the juices don't escape. Put the foil bag on the fire until the shells open. Remove, place in a bowl and serve with Asian butter: Melt 125g butter and add 2 tablespoons sweet chilli sauce, 2.5cm ginger, cut into julienned slivers, 2 spring onions, shredded, and a bunch of coriander, roughly chopped.

• Seafood Wraps

Grill a selection of fish on the fire - the best include organic salmon, halibut, mackerel, swordfish, trout, tuna. Make a salsa with 4 roughly chopped tomatoes; 1 clove garlic, minced; 1 diced avocado; 1 chilli, diced; chopped onion, to taste; some chopped coriander; salt, and the juice of one lime. Grill some flour tortillas and top each one with leaves, some salsa, a selection of the grilled fish and finally some crème fraîche.

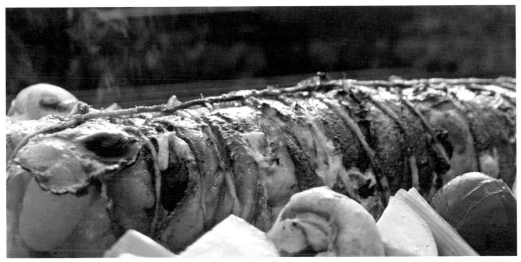

seafood barbecue

Tuna Burger

1kg fresh tuna (minced or diced finely with a sharp knife)
2cm ginger, grated
2 cloves garlic, minced
1/2 teaspoon cayenne pepper
1 teaspoon salt
1 tablespoon Dijon mustard

wasabi sauce:
1 tablespoon soy sauce
4 tablespoons rice vinegar
1 tablespoon mirin or sherry
6 tablespoons dashi
1 teaspoon wasabi paste

8 white bread rolls

Mince the tuna, either with a mincer or by dicing very finely. You could also pulse in a food processor, but don't let the mix get too mushy. Mix the burger ingredients together and, with wet hands, form into eight burgers.

Mix together the ingredients for the wasabi sauce.

Grill the burgers on the fire until the outside is crisp, but the inside is still moist. Serve in the rolls with a side bowl of wasabi sauce.

Cajun Marinated Sea Bass

Cajun marinade:

handful fresh fennel fronds, chopped
handful fresh thyme leaves
2 cloves garlic
½ teaspoon white peppercorns
½ teaspoon black peppercorns
½ teaspoon mustard seeds
½ teaspoon dried oregano
½ teaspoon cumin
¼ teaspoon cayenne pepper
1 teaspoon salt
1 tablespoon olive oil

4 whole sea bass

Make the marinade: chop the fennel, thyme and garlic. Pound the peppercorns and mustard seeds in a pestle. Combine all the marinade ingredients and stir well.

About one hour before cooking score the sea bass, and rub the marinade ingredients into the fish, inside and out. Leave for one hour, then cook on the barbecue for approximately 5 minutes each side.

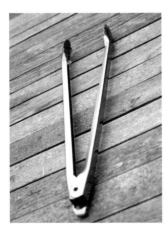

Seared Tuna Steak

honey and soy dressing:

½ **cup soy sauce**

½ **cup toasted sesame oil**

¼ **cup white wine vinegar**

½ **cup honey**

½ **clove garlic, minced**

4 tuna steaks (approximately 200g each)
olive oil
fresh herb salad (see page 35)
toasted sesame seeds

Place all the ingredients for the honey and soy dressing in a small pan and bring to the boil. Boil until the sauce is reduced and thickened (it should coat the back of a spoon). Reserve while you cook the tuna.

Brush the tuna with olive oil and grill or barbecue over a high heat. Don't overcook it, or it will become dry.

Serve with rice, topping the tuna with some honey and soy dressing, a handful of herb salad and some toasted sesame seeds.

seafood barbecue

seafood barbecue

Coral Butter

This butter is made from the corals of scallops. A good recipe for the scallops themselves is to marinate in some lemon juice and olive oil and skewer with some cucumber that has been seeded and diced, blanched and marinated with the scallops.

½ cup white wine
1 cup water
½ a carrot, sliced
1 an onion, roughly sliced
a sprig of dill and parsley
6 large scallop corals
125g butter
40ml cream

Mix the white wine and water into a small saucepan. Add the carrot, onion, dill and parsley and bring the mixture to a boil. Simmer for a few minutes, then add the scallop chorals. Simmer for 4-5 minutes. Remove the corals and reserve. Strain the liquid, discarding the aromatics.
Put the liquid back on the heat and boil until it has reduced to a little more than a tablespoon. Push the scallop corals through a plastic sieve. Place the corals, poaching liquid, butter and cream into a food processor and blend until smooth. Serve with some grilled scallops, or spooned over a peice of barbecued white fish.

seafood barbecue

fish for dinner

Oysters Tartare

This is an oyster dish for people who imagine they don't like oysters.

12 oysters

tomato and avocado salsa:
4 ripe vine tomatoes, deseeded and diced
1 large avocado, finely diced
1 small red onion, finely diced
1 clove garlic, finely chopped
60ml good olive oil
squeeze lemon juice
the juice of 1 lime
½ bunch coriander, stalks and all, roughly chopped
salt and pepper to taste

To make the salsa, place all the ingredients in a bowl. Mix gently so as not to break up the avocado pieces. Open the oysters and remove the mollusc from the shell, reserving the juice. Carefully chop the oysters into small dice. Strain the oyster juice into the salsa, and stir in the cubed oysters, very carefully. Chill in the fridge for an hour.

When ready to serve, spoon carefully back into the half oyster shells. Garnish with a sprig of coriander. Make sure to serve very cold.

Stuffed Courgette Flower Tempura

1 cup mascarpone
1 cup white crab meat
juice of ½ a lemon
salt and pepper
6 courgette flowers

tempura batter:
¾ cup plain flour
½ cup cornflour
sparkling water

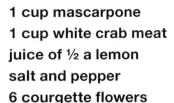

Mix together the mascarpone and crab, lemon juice and seasoning.

Blanch the courgette flowers in salted water for a few seconds, and then plunge into iced water to refresh. Carefully remove the stamens and spoon a little crab mixture into each of them. Fold the petals over to close.

Preheat the cooking oil to 180°C. Make the tempura batter just before you use it: mix flours with just enough water to make a batter with a fork. Stir the mixture until only just combined (it should, in fact, still be a bit lumpy - overmixing will make the batter tough).

Dip the flowers into the batter and deep fry in hot oil until just browned. Serve with a summer salad.

Grilled Scallops in their shell

with Anchovy and Lime Vinaigrette

Scallops are no longer sold in their shells by fishmongers - so you will need to order the shells in advance.

12 scallops

vinaigrette:
1 clove garlic, minced
4 anchovies
juice of two limes
100ml olive oil

Turn the grill on to maximum and preheat for at least 15 minutes to get it really hot. Brush four scallop shells with oil, and place the scallops back inside - placing three scallops in each half shell. Grill until the fish is just blistered (the timing of this will depend on the heat of your grill). Mix together the vinaigrette ingredients, spoon over the scallops and serve from the shell.

Seared Monkfish

with Black Pudding Stew

~~~~~~~

Once monkfish tails have been skinned they have an inner membrane covering the flesh. This has to be removed, or it curls up like an over-heated elastic band and causes the fish to become misshapen and cook un-evenly. You can do this at home, but any fishmonger would expect to do it for you. All you have to do is ask.

50ml olive oil
2 onions, sliced
pinch cayenne
pinch cinnamon
150ml white wine
8 ripe tomatoes, skinned, seeded and
  chopped
200g black pudding, skinned and sliced
finely chopped parsley
800g monkfish, cut into supremes
salt and pepper

Heat the olive oil on a medium heat and sweat the onions with the cayenne and cinnamon. Cook until just soft, then add the white wine. Turn up the heat and boil to reduce. When thickened, turn down the heat and add the tomatoes. Simmer for about 15 minutes until the tomatoes come together to make a sauce. Finally, add the black pudding and parsley. Turn the heat down and keep warm while you cook the monkfish. Season the monkfish with salt and pepper. Brush with oil and cook on a very high heat in a dry pan for three minutes each side. Squeeze over some lemon juice and add to the stew. Serve immediately.

Oven-baked Plaice

with Caper Butter

~~~~~~~~

Alternatives to plaice in this recipe could be another flat fish: lemon sole, witch, sea bream, John Dory. Or a round fish, in which case buy medium-sized fish and ask for them on the bone - red mullet, arctic char or haddock.

4 whole plaice, 400g each
olive oil for brushing

caper butter:
1 tablespoon olive oil
2 shallots, diced
1 clove garlic, minced
80g capers
125g butter
juice of 1 lemon
flat leaf parsley
freshly ground black pepper

Make the caper butter: heat the olive oil in a pan and add the diced shallots. Cook until soft, adding the garlic towards the end of cooking. Add the drained capers and the butter. Cook, stirring until the butter has melted, then stir in the lemon juice, pepper and parsley.

Cook the plaice: pre-heat your oven to its maximumum temperature, and place a baking tray into the oven while it is heating. Brush the plaice all over with olive oil and place on the hot baking tray. Bake the fish in the oven for 12 minutes. Carefully transfer the fish with all its juices to four warmed plates. Pour over some caper butter and serve.

Pan-Fried Haddock

with Creamed Celeriac, Crispy Potatoes and Salsa Verde

Look for thick fillets of haddock, taken from the top end of the fish, and ask your fishmonger to take out the little line of pin bones that run down the side of the fillet.

You could make this recipe with a centre piece of cod as well.

4 fillets of haddock (each
  around 200g)
seasoned flour
oil for frying

creamed celeriac:
1 celeriac, peeled with a knife
  and cut into small cubes
a knob butter
¼ cup cream
salt and pepper

To cook the celeriac: cook in boiling salted water until tender. Reserve cooking water. Put into a food processor and process with a third of a cup of cooking water and the same amount of cream until you get a purée.

Dip the haddock into seasoned flour and then pan fry in a little oil. Serve with the creamed celeriac and the salsa verde (see opposite).

Salsa Verde

1 bunch flat-leaf parsley
a few leaves of basil and mint
1 clove garlic, minced
1 teaspoon Dijon mustard
1 tablespoon capers
4 anchovy fillets, chopped
200ml olive oil
salt and pepper

Using a food processor pulse together the herbs, garlic, mustard, capers and anchovies. Keep the motor running and pour in the olive oil in a slow stream. Season to taste.

fish for dinner

Pan-Fried Monkfish

with Broccoli and Toasted Almonds, and Lemon Butter

4 pieces monkfish (each around 200g)
seasoned flour and oil for frying

1 head broccoli
2 tablespoons flaked almonds
Lemon Butter Sauce (see page 25)

sun-dried tomato pesto:
100g semi sun-dried tomatoes, chopped
4 anchovy fillets, chopped
200ml olive oil
1 tablespoon balsamic vinegar
1 clove garlic, minced
handful basil and a few mint leaves

Put all the sun-dried tomato pesto ingredients into a food processer and pulse to a lumpy purée. Toast the almonds in a hot dry frying pan, being very careful because they burn easily.

To assemble the dish, cook the broccoli in boiling salted water. Dip the monkfish into seasoned flour and pan fry in oil. Carefully heat the lemon butter sauce - don't heat too quickly or it might curdle. Assemble the fish and broccoli on a plate and drizzle over lemon butter sauce, and sprinkle on toasted almonds. Serve with a pot of sun-dried tomato pesto.

The monkfish here has been sliced into long pieces, at an angle which helps to cook evenly.

Lobster

with Drawn Butter

*Go on – treat yourself!
Cooking a lobster in your
own kitchen is one of life's
great experiences. Try
it at least once, and you
won't find it as difficult
as you might expect!*

1 lobster per person
salt and pepper
50g butter for each serving
lemon

Put a very large pan of water on to boil and cook the lobster for eight minutes. Take out of the pot, using tongs. When cool enough to handle twist the head off the lobster (this will make a very good stock) and cut the tail in half lengthways. Remove the meat from the claws and place inside the lobster tail. Season the lobster with salt and pepper.

To make the drawn butter, put a ramekin of butter into the microwave for 30 seconds to melt (use a saucepan on the heat, if you don't have a microwave).

Serve the lobster with a little pot of drawn butter and the lemon, cut in half.

*Drawn butter is also a good accompaniment for
Dover Sole cooked on the bone.*

Hake with
Roast Butternut Squash & Chorizo Risotto

If you put a squash in the microwave for a couple of seconds it makes it a lot easier to peel.

for the risotto:

1 butternut squash
2 tablespoons olive oil
1 onion, diced
fresh thyme leaves
300g risotto rice
1 litre chicken stock
2 tablespoons mascarpone cheese
1 fresh chorizo sausage, diced

4 pieces of monkfish (around 200g each)
seasoned flour
oil and butter for frying

First make the risotto: peel the squash and slice into large pieces. Roast in a 200°C oven for half an hour. Heat the olive oil in a saucepan and cook the onion and thyme for a few minutes before adding the rice. Heat the stock in another saucepan. Stir to coat the rice in the olive oil and then begin adding the stock. Add the stock a ladleful at a time, stirring between each ladleful until the liquid has been absorbed. When the rice is cooked and has absorbed all the liquid, stir in the mascarpone cheese. Finally stir in the diced sausage.

Slice the monkfish at an angle into long slices. Dip into seasoned flour and pan fry in a little butter and oil. Serve with the risotto.

Prawn Spaghetti
with Broccoli and Sweet Garlic Cream

2 heads of broccoli, separated into florets
450g spaghetti
500g prawns
olive oil for frying

For the sweet garlic cream:
1 head garlic
1 tablespoon olive oil
1 cup cream
knob of butter
salt and pepper
4 handfuls of rocket or watercress

Preheat the oven to 180°C. Place the whole head of garlic onto a piece of kitchen foil, drizzle with a little olive oil, wrap up and roast in the oven for 40 minutes, until soft but not browned. When cooked, pop out the soft garlic from the husks and pound in a pestle and mortar. You should have about 2 tablespoons garlic purée. Place the purée into a small saucepan and pour in the cream. Add a knob of butter and season. Bring the mixture to a simmer, stirring until it comes together to make a sauce. Bring a large pot of salted water to a rolling boil. Drop in the broccoli florets and cook for two minutes, until bright green. Remove with a slotted spoon. Use the same water to cook the pasta. Two minutes before the end of pasta cooking time, sauté the prawns in olive oil. Add the broccoli and the sweet garlic cream and cook for two minutes before adding the strained spaghetti. Divide into four bowls.

Roast Cod
with parsley mash

You could substitute any fish from the cod family for this dish, especially ling or white pollack.

parsley mash:
20g parsley, chopped
¼ cup olive oil
8-10 potatoes, peeled
salt and pepper

4 portions of thickly-cut fresh cod fillets
salt and pepper
2 tablespoons olive oil

Blend the parsley and olive oil in a food processor. Boil and mash the potatoes and whisk in the parsley oil and season. Preheat the oven to its maximum temperature. Place an ovenproof pan on a high heat, and leave for 5 minutes until the pan is hot. Season the fish with salt and pepper. Add the olive oil to the pan; it should glisten and cover the base of the pan with a glossy film of very hot oil. Place the fish onto this searing heat, and cook for 2-3 minutes. Place the whole pan in the oven for a further 2-3 minutes until the fish is milky white and firm to the touch.

You can serve this garnished with a tomato salsa. (See page 24)

Arctic Charr

with Beetroot and Apple Stew

Arctic charr is from the same family as trout and salmon. It's both a fresh water and seawater fish, with a meaty flesh and a sweet earthy taste. Farmed Arctic charr is now available all year round in Ireland. See www.cloonacoolarcticcharr.ie *for details.*

4 raw beetroots
1 tablespoon olive oil
¼ cup balsamic vinegar
1 tablespoon honey
1 cooking apple
salt and pepper

4 fillets Arctic charr
olive oil

1 tablespoon grated horseradish mixed with
¼ cup of pouring cream, salt and pepper.

Peel the beetroots whilst still raw. Cut into wedges and place on a roasting dish. Drizzle over some olive oil, balsamic vinegar and the honey. Peel, core and slice the apples and place on top. Season with salt and pepper. Cover the dish with foil and put in an oven, preheated to 190°C for an hour, until the beetroot is soft and the apple has distintegrated into a sweet sauce.

Rub the fillets of charr with olive oil and place under a hot grill. Grill, flesh side up for 6-8 minutes. Serve with the beetroot relish, and drizzle a little bit of horseradish sauce around.

Salt and Chilli Squid

750g squid
50g rice flour
50g potato flour
2 teaspoons salt
1 teaspoon Sichuan peppercorns, crushed
oil for deep frying
sweet chilli sauce

Slice the squid into fine rings. Combine the flours and seasoning on a plate. Heat the oil to 170°C.

Dredge the squid in the seasoned flour, shake off the excess and immediately deep fry. Do this in batches. Drain the squid on kitchen paper and serve immediately with Sweet Chilli Sauce.

Red Gurnard
with Savoy Cabbage

You could also use Grey Gurnard, which is a lesser used, but equally delicious fish.

olive oil
1 onion, diced
1 savoy cabbage, sliced
2 cloves garlic, minced
4 fillets of red gurnard
seasoned flour
more olive oil for cooking

Heat the olive oil in a saucepan and add the onion and garlic. Cook until soft. Add the cabbage and a glass of water and, using a combination of steam and braising, cook the cabbage, which will take around 10 minutes.

When you are ready to serve, dip the fish in the seasoned flour and pan fry in a hot pan. Serve with the cabbage and some sautéed potatoes.

fish for dinner

Battered White Pollack with marrowfat peas

1 box marrowfat peas
1 shallot, very finely chopped
1 clove garlic, finely chopped
mixture of chopped green herbs, eg parsley
  thyme, celery leaves, sage, marjoram
salt and pepper
1 tablespoon extra virgin olive oil

1 tablespoon dried yeast granules
300ml beer
225g flour
salt
4 large fillets white pollack

First make the marrowfat pea purée: The peas will probably come with a tablet of soda, steep them with the soaking tablet overnight in boiling water. Rinse and place peas in a saucepan. Cover with water and simmer for about 20 minutes. Season, stir in the shallot, garlic, chopped herbs, olive oil and season. To make the batter: dissolve the yeast in the beer and leave to settle for about 10 minutes. Sift the flour and salt into a bowl and make a well in the centre. Pour in the yeasted beer, stir well to get rid of any lumps, then leave for an hour to prove. Dip the pieces of pollack into the batter and deep fry at 170°C until the batter is golden and the fish cooked. Serve with the herbed peas.

fish for dinner

Ray with Sun-dried Tomato and Spinach Risotto

It is essential to buy the ray skinned, and a kind and helpful fishmonger will bone it for you as well.

3 cloves garlic
4 tablespoons olive oil
500g spinach
1 litre vegetable stock
1 onion, diced
vermouth
300g risotto rice
3 tomatoes, peeled, seeded and diced

2 ray, skinned and boned
seasoned flour
olive oil

Blanch the spinach in boiling salted water for a few seconds. Drain. Heat 1 tablespoon olive oil in a large saucepan and add the garlic. Cook over a low heat until soft. Add the spinach and combine with the garlic oil. Remove from the pan and purée in a food processor. Heat the stock. Heat the remaining olive oil in the large sauce-pan, and cook the onion until soft. Splash in a half glass of vermouth and then add the rice. Stir to coat the grains, and then add the stock, one ladle at a time, waiting until each ladle is absorbed before adding the next one. When the rice is cooked and all the liquid is absorbed add the spinach purée and the diced tomato. Dip the ray pieces into seasoned flour and pan fry in a little olive oil. Serve with the risotto.

Baked John Dory
with Tapenade

This is one for the summer deck. Buy a good tapenade, make a salad and keep it simple.

**2 large John Dory, on the bone
olive oil, salt and pepper, butter
tapenade**

Dry the fish and place on a roasting tray. Brush liberally with the olive oil and season. Add a few knobs of butter and bake in the oven, preheated to 180°C for about 18 minutes. Serve the fish straight from the roasting tray with some tapenade and a vine tomato salad.

fish for dinner

Casserole of Red Gurnard
with Prawns in a Tarragon Cream

300g gurnard, cut into strips
300g prawns, peeled
1 tablespoon olive oil

tarragon cream:
700ml fish stock
250ml cream
1 onion, finely diced
knob of butter
1/3 cup white wine vinegar
25g flour and 25g soft butter
1 handful fresh French tarragon,
  chopped

To make the tarragon cream: boil together the fish stock and the cream until slightly thickened. In a separate pan sauté the onion in a knob of butter. Add the white wine vinegar and boil until the vinegar has almost evaporated. Add the stock/cream mixture and heat again. Mix together the 25g of flour and soft butter. Have the creamy stock on a high simmer whilst you whisk in spoonfuls of this flour/butter mixture. The sauce will thicken into a smooth velouté. Add the chopped tarragon. When ready to serve, preheat the oven to 170°C. If you have individual ovenproof casseroles, use these for this dish. Otherwise use just one. Sauté the fish in the olive oil for 2 minutes, then place the fish and prawns carefully onto the bottom of each casserole. Pour over the tarragon cream. The mixture should be quite saucy, with the pieces of fish sitting in a bath of the tarragon cream. Finish the casserole off in the oven for 4-5 minutes. Serve with rice.

The Irish Association of Seafood Companies

The Irish Association of Seafood Companies (IASC) develops, promotes and represents the interests of independent seafood retailers and processors in Ireland.

All IASC members have an unrivalled knowledge of seafood. Not only will they skin, bone or fillet your favourite fresh fish for you, they're more than happy to take the time to offer advice on recipe ideas, proper preparation and serving tips.

So, if you're looking for the very best in seafood, simply call into any IASC member.

IASC
70B Clanbrassil Street
Dundalk
Co Louth

Tel: 042-938 6977

Irish Association of
Seafood Companies

Nobody knows more about seafood
www.iasc.ie

Belvelly Smokehouse

Cobh, Cork,
Co Cork

Tel: 021 4811089
www.frankhederman.com

Contact Frank Hederman

Open - Midleton Market 9am-
1pm Sat, Cobh market 10am-
noon Fri, Smokehouse shop
open Mon-Sat 10am-5.30pm

Belvelly Smokehouse is the oldest traditional smokehouse in Ireland. With his smoked fish recognised internationally as a superb premium product, Frank Hederman has himself quickly become one of the starchitects of Ireland's emergence as a distinctive food destination, and no food writer's itinerary is complete without a visit to Cobh. Their impressive list of customers include Ballymaloe House, Richard Corrigan and Selfridges, and their Ditty's Irish Smoked Oatcakes are available from Waitrose and Fortnum & Mason. This year a new range of Mrs Hederman's fish pies, chowders and fish cakes has seen an enthusiastic response from their devoted customers. Meanwhile the shop at the smoke house sells a range of savoury and sweet biscuits and specialist teas from Suki teas in Belfast. There is also good olive oil and pasta, jams and chutneys and other home-made foods and smoked goods. There is nothing else quite like smoked haddock straight from the Belvelly smokehouse.

Central Fish Market

New Street,
Bantry,
Co Cork

Tel: 027 53714

Contact Colman Keohane

Open 10am-5.30pm Mon, 9am-
6pm Tue-Fri, 9.30am-5.30pm
Sat

Colman Keohane revived an old tradition in Bantry when he opened the Central Fish Market. In the past there had always been a fish shop in the town, but the tradition had been allowed to die. Colman, with a family background in fish and shellfish, was just the man to bring fresh fish to Bantry for the new century.

"My father is in the business, he is involved in Bantry Bay Seafoods, and I always had a background in fish. As a kid I was always experimenting. I knew I wanted to work with fish, and I experimented with prawns, mussels and finally opened this fresh fish shop in Bantry."

A natural progression in 2008 saw Colman and his sister Ann-Marie open The Fish Kitchen, a lovely fish restaurant which is – literally – over the shop.

"Our ethos in the restaurant is the same as the shop. Keep it very simple, very fresh, make it fun and casual, and concentrate on quality."

Dennehy's Seafood

96 Great William
O'Brien St,
Blackpool,
Cork, Co Cork

Tel: 021 4302144

Contact Tom Dennehy

Open 8am-5.30pm Mon-Fri

Tom Dennehy runs the shop that his father, Tom senior, opened more than 60 years ago, and today he still buys all the fish himself from nearby Union Hall. "I sell the ordinary everyday fish, like whiting, plaice, sole, cod and haddock, rather than the prime fish, and I find there's a great demand for it."

Tom also extols the virtues of the system retailers have of being able to buy their fish at auction. "You can choose exactly what you want, rather than just phoning somebody up. You can find excellent quality through this system."

"It's a tough business" he says, and whilst "it can be cold, it can be miserable, but it's in your blood." It's in the blood, alright.

Fishy Fishy Shop

Guardwell, Kinsale,
Co Cork

Tel: 021 4774453

Contact Martin Shanahan

Open noon-5pm Tue-Sat

Martin Shanahan, author of this book, operates a fish shop in Kinsale as well as the internationally renowned Fishy Fishy Café. 2009 sees new plans for the store, which will continue to operate as an excellent fish shop, but will also feature a fish and chip café. Customers can sit down or take-away home-made fresh fish, deep-fried in their famously light batter, along with potato wedges. The food, including chowders and fish cakes will be served in disposable cups and plates – and the quality will be stellar. Wines will be available by the glass and the seating will be communal. The food will be delicious, and the character will never veer away from the fact that this is a fish shop.

Kay O'Connell

13-20 Grand
Parade Market,
Cork, Co Cork

Tel: 021 4276380
www.koconnellsfish.com

Contact Pat & Paul O'Connell

Open 7.30am-6pm Mon-Sat

"Anything that comes from Cork is always great quality!" says Pat O'Connell, the uniquely colourful, eminently quotable raconteur who – when he isn't getting his picture taken with visiting dignitaries who call into the market – sells the finest fish from the impressive Kay O'Connell fish stall in Cork's legendary English Market.

The stall was started, almost 50 years ago, by Kathleen O'Connell, and since her death, the brothers Paul and Pat O'Connell have continued the tradition of selling what must be one of the most diverse and exciting ranges of fish in the whole country.

They have patiently and purposefully expanded the stall and the range of fish they sell, so if you are a Polish guy in search of carp or a Japanese girl in search of sushi and sashimi, you are in the right place.

If you are an Irish food lover, then take the brothers' advice as to what is best on the day and you will be delighted by their suggestions.

Yawl Bay Seafoods

Youghal,
Co Cork
www.yawlbayseafood.ie
Tel: 024 92290

Contact David Browne

Open 9am-5pm Mon-Fri,
10am-2pm Sat (limited hours off
season)

Yawl Bay Seafoods began life 21 years ago in a small cottage in Youghal in County Cork. The business was started by Jim Browne, father of the current owner, David. "The business really started over a bet my father made comparing Irish to Norwegian smoked salmon. He said Irish was better, and his Norwegian friend is still a regular customer!" Since then, the company has moved three times, but are now "where we want to be in a state-of-the art facility".

The flagship product of Yawl Bay is their smoked salmon which is sold in its distinctive Celtic design package and exported all over the world. They also produce a very superior smoked haddock. "It's my favourite fish," says David Browne. "It's underrated, but it has huge versatility. I love it skinned, then wrapped in bacon and baked."

As well as the distinguished smoked fish, Yawl Bay Seafoods has a factory shop which is worth crossing the country to visit. The ethos of the company is to buy large, thick fillets of fish and "value for money" is another operating principle of Yawl Bay.

"I don't fill up my counter with all types of fish, I just sell fish you can get at a reasonable price. And, at the end of the day, if the customer comes back and says 'Jaysus, that was lovely', well there's huge self-fulfilment in that."

Daly's Seafoods

Cahirciveen,
Co Kerry

Tel: 066 947 2082

Main Street, Castleisland
Tel: 066 7142799

Main Street, Abbeyfeale
Tel: 068 31974
Contact Michael Daly

Open 9am-6pm Mon-Sat

Daly's is a first-generation business, started by Michael and Kathleen Daly. Michael was a fisherman in the seventies, so there is an expertise underpinning their work, and their success to date has been swiftly achieved. The company operates a state-of-the-art factory in Cahirciveen where they smoke and barbecue salmon and other seafood, and process fresh fish. In addition to this they run two fine shops. The fish is sourced from Portmagee, Castletownbere and Union Hall.

Duinin Seafoods

Market Place,
Tralee, Co Kerry

Tel: 066 7121026

Contact Paddy O'Mahony

Open 9am-6pm Mon-Sat

Paddy O'Mahony knows fish, and, listening to his lyrical Kerry tones, one senses an epicurean gourmet at the heart of all his many business endeavours. In the late sixties Mr O'Mahony was the manager of the Dingle Fishermens' Co-Op and in the eighties he opened Ballyhea Fisheries, where his fish processing still takes place.

The O'Mahony's shop in Market Place in Tralee has sold fish for the last 22 years, and along with fresh fillets, they make, sell and export various smoked fish including salmon, mackerel and, seasonally, haddock, cod, whiting and tuna.

The O'Mahonys also own and run the Meadowlands Hotel in Tralee, a hotel where, in both the restaurant and bar, guests are treated to the freshest of seafood. They know it's fresh because the owners catch it themselves.

For someone who has been in the industry for a number of years, Paddy O'Mahony is positive about the fish he can sell. "Fish is handled better now. Irish fishermen today know more about handling than they ever used to. So even though we used to be able to buy from day boats, where the fish was only a couple of hours out of the water, but now they have to travel hours to get the fish they cool it down immediately it is caught - it's handled properly on the boat. The first couple of hours after a fish is caught is the most important. And if it's handled well then it keeps fresh."

Spillanes Seafood

Lackavan, Killarney,
Co Kerry

Tel: 064 31320

Open 9am-6pm Mon-Fri (closed for lunch), 9am-1pm Sat

Contact Paudie Spillane

The Kerry institution that is Spillane's Seafood was started by Michael Spillane "almost by accident", according to his son Paudie, who is now at the helm. "My father was managing the fishermens' co-op in Cromane and the Hotel Europe asked him if he could bring them back a bit of fish." This was in the days when Killarney was at the pinnacle of European tourism. Families would come to the hotel from Germany and other parts of Europe and stay for a month. "The quality of food they would offer was mind-blowing. There were stories of putting out 300 lobsters on a Saturday night." This is the elegant pedigree that has made Spillane's such a huge part of the retail and wholesale life of Killarney. The Spillane's reputation is international. This is where Rachel Allen sources her fish when shooting her TV series.

"We have our regulars," says Paudie, modestly. Nowadays the company is first and foremost a fish processing and wholesaling enterprise, but regulars know that if you turn up at their shop in the factory there will be probably 50 or 60 different species of fish on offer, all of it as fresh as they would expect, and good value. Paudie obviously relishes the business, "we may have good days and bad days, but no two days are the same." And, even though the hours may be long "if you do a job, you might as well do it right."

GJ Sadlier Seafoods

2 Roches Street
Limerick, Co Limerick

Tel: 061 414232

Contact John Sadlier

Open 8.30am-5.45pm Tue-Sat

The history of Sadlier's is long and distinguished: John's parents, Jim and Susan, opened the original shop on Henry Street back in 1948, moving four years later to Roches Street where they have been ever since.
In the early days they specialised in poultry and rabbits, and started to sell fish when they moved to Roches Street. Today, health regulations no longer permit them to sell rabbits, but sales of Irish poultry are still a strong feature of the shop.
John Sadlier himself came into the business in 1974, a "young gossoon of 16", and has developed the business to a point where sales and turnover have increased steadily and successfully year-on-year. Today cod and salmon are the best sellers, "but with people travelling there is also demand for sea bass, swordfish, tuna". Former best-sellers such as whiting have declined in popularity, but John says a keen cost-consciousness is seeing people choose haddock and other sometimes overlooked fish.

René Cusack

Raheen, Limerick

Tel: 061 317566

Retail Shops:
St Alfonsus Street, Limerick
Tel: 061 440054
Open 9am-5.30pm Mon-Sat

Milk Market
Tel: 061 408011
Open 10am-6pm Tue-Sat

9 Market Street, Ennis
Tel: 061 6892712
Open 9am-6pm Mon-Sat

Belhavel, Athlone
Tel: 0906 420355
Open 10am-6pm

Contact Paul Cusack

The fish shops now known as René Cusack began life as the Grimsby Fish Stores, started by Michael Cusack in 1910. His store was named after the UK port from which Michael imported most of his fish - the Irish fishing industry having been brought to its knees by the taxes on exports of Irish fish.

This display of business acumen seemed to run in the family, and by the time René Cusack had taken control the fishing industry in Ireland was thriving, and René and his wife Olive Cusack expanded the premises on the Dock Road.

Today the business is in the hands of affable and capable Paul Cusack, and there are four René Cusack stores, all hosting a fantastic display of fish. The fish processing business is in Raheen, where they process fish and smoke salmon in the traditional way. The philosophy behind the stores hasn't changed. "I want to make shopping here as pleasurable an experience as I can, and then people come back," says Paul Cusack. "Anybody can buy whiting and put it on a counter, but if you have a good approach to the customer, if you personalise it, and give time to your customers, then it becomes a cultural thing."

If you're in Limerick on a Saturday morning, don't miss the Saturday morning market, and René Cusack's fish counter. As Paul Cusack says, "It's a fun place, it's buzzing!"

Burren Smokehouse

Birgitta and Peter Curtin are amongst the leading fish smokers in Ireland. Their Burren Smokehouse specialises in delicate, expertly-smoked salmon, trout, mackerel and eel, which is available throughout the country, as well as from their funky food and craft shop in Lisdoonvarna, where they also sell a small supply of white fish.

The shop also operates a visitor's centre, and Birgitta and Peter supply a wide range of very desirable hampers featuring their smokehouse products as well as other local artisan foods, which they distribute all around the globe.

Their pub, The Roadside Tavern, just up the road towards the town also serves good food, and has lively sessions.

Kinkora Road, Lisdoonvarna, Co Clare

Tel: 065 7074432
www.burrensmokehouse.ie

Contact Birgitta Hedin-Curtin

Open daily, summer 9am-6pm, winter 10am-5pm

Sea Lyons Seafood Sales

Carrigaholt,
Co Limerick

Tel: 065 905 8222

Contact Gearoid Lyons

Open 9am-6pm Mon-Sat (till 5pm on Saturdays)

Ask Gearoid Lyons about the fishing industry and he says, simply: "We eat, drink and live it". Mr Lyons is a man who has spent 27 years working with seafood, initially working on trawlers, before he and his family settled in Carrigaholt, "a coastal community at the mouth of the river Shannon", where Sea Lyons Seafood Sales has its headquarters. He no longer works the trawlers, but "my kids and friends are still involved."

In addition to the Sea Lyons factory shop in Carrigaholt, they also run fish vans in counties Clare, Limerick and Kerry and do a home delivery service for those in their catchment area. As Gearoid says, "fish and fishing is part of our whole life".

The Fish Market

19 Lwr Market St,
Ennis, Co Clare

Tel: 065 6842424

Contact Val Egan

Open 9am-6pm Tue-Fri, 9am-1pm Sat

The Fish Market opened its doors in 1997, and it has not changed since the day it opened, with the original fishmonger, Val Egan, still running the business. Mr Egan works in partnership with Garrihy's Seafoods in Doolin, and that company enjoys a long tradition - no less than three generations - of business, processing and selling fish and seafood in County Clare.

Eamon Garrihy now directs business in Garrihy's Seafoods, taking over from his uncle, Donie, and his grandfather before that. "I know my list off by heart" he says, reeling off each and every fish he sells in his lyrical Clare accent. Garrihy's now has a new 3,000-square foot processing plant, which helps them to present the fish at its best.

Mr Garrihy believes chefs have had an influence on people's taste, with their diverse requests, and that as a result fish like tuna and swordfish are now popular alongside the well learned list of their specialities. Most of their fish are sourced from Rossaveal, and as well as the white fish they offer lobsters, oysters, prawns, mussels and clams.

The Fish Market shop has a dedicated customer base, a long-lived, traditional shop in this fine and handsome market town.

Connemara Smokehouse

Bunowen Pier
Ballyconneely
Co Galway

Tel: 095 23739

www.smokehouse.ie

Contact Graham and Saoirse
Roberts

Open 9am-5pm Mon-Fri
(closed 1pm-2pm)

Graham Roberts' impressive operation goes from strength to strength every year. It's no surprise, for the foundations of Connemara Smokehouse are as sound as they come.

First of all, it's a family business. Graham Roberts, who is today at the helm of the Connemara Smokehouse, has taken an active role in the business all his working life, "from as soon as I left school. It was what I wanted to do." Graham's father had his own fishing boat, and was instrumental, with Graham, in developing an environmentally friendly way of catching tuna with BIM, the Irish Fisheries Board. Tuna today is one of their flagship products. They cold smoke it – and you will see this cold smoked tuna on many notable restaurant menus, including Rick Stein's restaurants in Padstow. They also honey roast smoke it, and most recently have begun to make a smoked tuna mousse, which comes from a recipe from Graham's grandmother.

The Connemara Smokehouse pride themselves in being specialists in wild, organic and environmentally sustainable products. They sell smoked salmon, mackerel and trout, and, when available, smoked cod and kippers. Graham Roberts still hand fillets every fish, and everything is extra carefully produced. "I like to keep my hand on everything, because that's where quality comes from."

The internet is now a large part of the business, with customers able to buy online, and as well as that they open the smokehouse to the public. Often customers will start by calling in to buy for a picnic, and follow up with mail order.

Deacy's Fish Shop

11 High Street,
Galway, Co Galway

Tel: 091 562515

Contact Michael Deacy

Open 9am-6pm Mon-Sat

Michael Deacy is the fourth generation of his family to run Deacy's Fish Shop and his children have just started to work with him, so a fifth generation will take over this Galway institution in time. Deacy's has been on High Street since 1915, a street where traditionally fish was sold from stalls. In fact the premises that is now Deacy's Fish Shop was originally a record and music shop, with a fish counter outside, and the family lived upstairs above the shop. There would have been a number of fish counters running the length of the street, so this is a place of historical significance for fish selling in Galway.

Michael Deacy has worked in Deacy's since he left college in 1979. Much has changed in the selling of fish, according to Michael. "Fish was always, always sold on the bone," he says. But our tastes now, he says are for no bone and no skin. Historically, however, there would have been much less choice "Brill used to be thrown in as plaice, and there was no such thing as monkfish - the French taught us about that, and taught us the price as well!"

Duane's Seafood

Duane's Fish Market
Ballybane Industrial Estate,
Galway, Co Galway
Tel: 086 6044097
Open 10am-6pm Tue-Sat

Duane's Fish Market
67 Henry Street,
Galway, Co Galway
Tel: 091 586641
Open 7am-5pm Mon-Sat

Oyster Creek,
Maree, Oranmore
Tel: 091 790499

Contact Thomas Duane
Tel: 086 6044097

Duane's Seafood offer their customers over 100 different varieties of fish daily. "We literally have everything"says Thomas Duane. The scope and variety of their produce stems from the fact that they wholesale to over 100 hotel and restaurant customers in the West of Ireland region, so customers at their newly aquired Henry Street shop can take advatage of the huge selection thanks to the many whims and demands of their many chefly customers.

The Duane family have been in the fish business for over sixty years, Thomas's grandfather having been a shell fish buyer and exporter. The firm now have a new 6000-sq ft factory in Ballybane Industrial Estate where they process their fish and also sell to the public from their smart new shop, in addition to the Henry Street shop.

The business still involves exporting as well as retailing - with the export of shellfish to France and Spain. The fish sold in the shops includes shellfish from Connemara, Clare Island salmon and fish bought in from Rossaveal, Skibbereen and Dingle. Duanes also operate a shellfish factory and purification plant in Oranmore. From here they supply their own domestic customers as well as exports of live shellfish to Europe.

"We pride ourselves in suppling very fresh fish at value for money prices and in a friendly professional manner and I'm on the end of the phone for anybody to answer any queries whether you're a housewife buying a fillet of mackerel or a foriegn customer buying a lorry load."

Ernie's Fish Stores

Sea Road, Galway,
Co Galway

Tel: 091 586812

Contact Ernest Deacy

Open 9am-6pm Mon-Sat

Ernie Deacy opened Ernie's Fish Stores some 34 years ago, selling a comprehensive range of seafood at the stellar standard that you could and would expect from someone born into a family of seafod experts - Ernie's great grand aunt, Mary Joe Conroy, was the biggest exporter of herrings in Ireland, way back in the 1890s.

Ernie's, as it is today, started life as a smart clothes shop, McCormack's. Deacy's took over and opened, selling fish, fruit and vegetables. It stayed with this successful format for over 20 years, but in the last decade it changed again to encompass modern tastes and to cater for the demands of a changing audience. Along with Fair Trade goods and organic wines and produce, there is now a huge selection of specialist teas and coffees to choose from, as well as a range of spices and herbs.

Ernest Deacy is adept at reading his audience, and adept at changing with the times when it's needed. And, in keeping with family tradition, the next generation has already started work at Deacy's, with both Ernie's son and daughter working alongside him. And, more than a century after the family started the business, you can still buy herring.

The Seafood Centre @ Galway Bay Seafoods

New Docks, Galway,
Co Galway

Tel: 091 563011

www.galwaybayseafoods.com

Contact Noel Holland

Open 8.15am-5pm Mon-Wed &
Sat, 8.15am-7.30pm Thu & Fri

The Seafood Centre developed organically from the thriving wholesale business of Galway Bay Seafoods. People would turn up at the door of the factory and plead for some of their very fresh fish. In response the family put out a little table, which turned into a little corner shop. This facility got busier and busier and developed into a factory shop. Then in 2007 it was transformed into a professional, modern shop "designed from our own heart and head to get every aspect of quality fish", says Noel Holland. Displaying probably an optimism that was possibly out of step with the time, the company built a nine-metre counter. "At the time it seemed mad", says Noel. But, it worked, thanks to being able to stock it well: "we try to focus on what the customer needs, we have a discerning customer who wants fresh fish from all over the world, allied to local produce."

In a sense, this progression was a coming back full circle to the Holland family roots. John V Holland started the business in 1950. It evolved from a fish shop to a wholesale fish processing business and today the focus is back on retail again with this handsome shop. "We're very proud of our quality" says Noel "it's our first, second and last thought of every day. But", he adds, "You're only as good as yesterday."

Gannet Fishmongers

32 Dun Ri,
Athenry, Co Galway

Tel: 086 3488591

Ballinasloe, Fri 9am-1pm,
Loughrea, Thu 9am-1pm,
Oranmore, Thur noon-6pm,
Moycullen, Fri noon-6pm,
Gort, Fri 10am-2pm,
Claregalway, Sat 10am-2pm,
Galway, Sat 9am-6pm.

Contact Stephane Griesbach

"People lose their head a bit when they see what we do", says Stephane Griesbach, accurately describing his joyful customers on first sight of his fantastic presentation of fish in the famous Galway Saturday Market. And no wonder, there's sometimes up to 500kg of fish on display, much of it sold on the bone. For Parisian-born M Griesbach understands that you eat first with the eyes.

Stephane Griesbach is an unusual entity in the fish business, for he's a first-generation fishmonger. He has, however, very quickly established a reputation as a superlative seller of fresh fish. "It's enthusiasm," he says, "people realise we are very serious about what we are doing. We work hard. We give cooking tips, and we have good prices."

Stephane came to Ireland in 1997, and, after working in the salmon farming business and other fish retailing operations, he saw potential in the Galway market, an opportunity which, he says, has put him on the retailing map.

Gannet Fishmongers now has a 3,000-square foot production unit, is venturing into wholesale, and enjoys a "good squad, all professional people" working for the company.

Ninety percent of the fish they sell comes from Ireland, and one of the things Stephane loves to do is "have some treats" for his customers, such as abalones or fresh tuna.

McDonagh's

22 Quay St, Galway,
Co Galway

Tel: 091 565001

Contact Colm McDonagh

Open 5pm-10pm Mon-Sat (restaurant), noon-11pm Mon-Sat, 4pm-10pm Sun (fish & chip bar)

Galway is one of those cities where everybody with any sort of a history in retailing claims to be not just a shop, but a veritable institution. In fact, McDonagh's genuinely is an institution in the city. A fish restaurant which also has a fish and chip bar, McDonagh's combines simplicity and reliability in their fish cookery to make not just a veritable institution, but also an essential address.

Gerry Blain Fish Sales

Carrick-on-Shannon,
Thurs 11am-2.30
Roscommon (behind Gleeson's Hotel), Fri 10am-3pm
Sligo Institute of Technology, Sat 9am-1pm

Tel: 087 1375516

Contact Gerry Blain

Also known as "The Donegal Fisherman" Gerry Blain was reared in a fishing family and has been a fisherman most of his life. In summer he still fishes from his own small boat, and these are the fish he sells in country markets in the North West. Meanwhile in winter he will select from the best that Killybegs and Greencastle have to offer.

Mackerel and hake are two of his most popular fish. "We sell mackerel caught with handliners from Jun-Oct, and the large mackerel from Killybegs boats in the winter. They have a bit of fat on them then which gives the best flavour."

Gerry also sells shellfish and a good range of locally caught fish. "It's a tradition in my family going back many years, fishing in small boats. And I love the markets. You can go direct to the customer, I enjoy that relationship. There's a bit of crack in it."

O'Reillys Fish Centre

23 Castle Street,
Ballyshannon,
Co Donegal

Tel: 071 9851389

Contact PJ O'Reilly

Open 9am-6pm Tue-Sat

For more than 100 years, and through three generations, O'Reilly's Fish Centre has been selling fresh fish in Ballyshannon. PJ O'Reilly has seen trends and politics come and go, and reckons very little has changed in the selling of fresh fish in Ireland. "When it was plentiful there was a rush to export, so fresh fish was always difficult to find." Nowadays he finds his customers are more health conscious, and despite the increased cost of sourcing it, fresh fish is more in demand than ever.

O'Reilly's is a traditional shop, which means that they sell fish in its correct season, and promote the fish that is best for each time of the year. "If you promote the fish that's in season, it tastes better," PJ says simply, "and then the customers will be happy." So in winter there's plump mackerel and herring, and in summer you'll find scrummy, lobster and crab claws. It's a simple, and noble, philosophy, and it sure makes for good shopping.

Clarke's Salmon Smokery

O'Rahilly St, Ballina,
Co Mayo
Tel: 096 21022

Peter St, Westport,
Co Mayo

Tel: 098 24379

www.clarkes.ie

Contact John, Dara or Kevin
Clarke

Open 9am-6pm Mon-Sat

Clarke's started life in 1945, when Jackie Clarke opened the business in Ballina, selling not only fish, but rabbits and chickens as well. The proximity of the salmon-stocked River Moy led the shop to go more and more in the direction of selling salmon, and in the eighties Clarke's became solely a fish retailer. The company always exported fresh wild salmon to England, and the exporting of smoked salmon took off in the seventies and eighties when local tourists took their catch back to France, Germany, Switzerland and other countries, and then reordered come Christmas.

The smokery was started in the sixties, and is just one of the reasons for Clarke's eminent reputation. The smoking still takes place today in the rear of the seafood deli in Ballina, using Jackie's original recipe. Clarke's salmon is recognised both locally and internationally as a superb smoked salmon, winning major retail and media awards and much critical acclaim.

Today the business is run by Jackie's sons, John, Dara and Kevin, and the business has taken a fresh turn in the new millennium with the rise of internet shopping, and exporting salmon through this medium is a substantial part of the business.

Their online shop sells and exports not only smoked salmon, but barbecued salmon, smoked silver eel and sea vegetables.

Nowadays Clarke's seafood delis are the very picture of a modern retailing operation. Their two well-designed, attractive stores stock a range of convenient, value-added, carefully made foods, including fishcakes, seafood lasagne, seafood pie, salmon en croute and various pâtés. The enterprising Clarke brothers have moved with the times, and the two Clarkes shops are two of the most dynamic retailing spaces in Ireland.

Ireland West Seafare

The Pier, Killala,
Co Mayo

Tel: 096 32717

Contact Niall Byrne

Open 9am-5pm Mon-Sat

Alongside prime fresh fish and wild salmon in season, this company specialises in crab and lobster. Many of the shop's customers are local restaurateurs.

Smack on the pier, here in Ireland's leading surfing county, the shop is easy to spot with its bright blue sign.

Recently the company have taken a new direction – they now sell at a large number of country markets, including Belmullet on Tues, Ballinrobe on Wed, and Castlebar, Longford and Sligo on Fri. Look out for their mobile unit, trading under the name of Ireland West Seafare, and selling quality fish.

Tiernan Brothers

Main Street, Foxford
Co Mayo

Tel: 094 9256731

www.themoy.com

Contact Michael and PJ Tiernan

Open 7 days during the summer season, 8am-6pm. Off season hours 9am-6pm Mon-Sat

The Tiernan Brothers' association with fishing and the River Moy can be traced back to Michael and PJ Tiernan's great-great grandfather Martin Tiernan. Martin Tiernan was one of the foremost Fly-Tiers in Ireland, and his great-great grandsons are today synonymous with angling in County Mayo.

Over the years the shop has changed direction. It began as a butcher, fish tackle shop and fishmonger, and remained a fishing tackle shop in the hands of the senior Tiernan Brothers, Michael and PJ's father and uncle.

In the mid 1990's Michael and PJ re-opened the tackle shop in Foxford, and the now-flourishing business spawned a fish shop. This was a natural progression, as the selling of tackle is a seasonal thing, whereas fresh fish has a market all year round.

Tiernan's is a traditional shop – "We have very little in the freezer, just fresh fish" says Martin. And alongside the fish shop they have a busy internet online store selling tackle, and they can also be found selling in local country markets: Foxford Woollen Mills, Sat 9am-2.30pm Charlestown, Murphy's Londis, Tues 9am-2pm Swinford Main Street, Thurs 9am-2pm Castlebar Market Square, Fri 9am-5pm

John Dory Fish Merchant

Strandhill,
Co Sligo

Tel: 087 648 9783

Contact Maura O'Boyle

Ballyhaunis, Co Mayo,
8am-3.45pm Wednesday
Ballaghaderreen, Co
Roscommon, 7.30am-5pm
Thursday
Castlerea, Co Roscommon,
7.30am-1pm Friday

"When I'm not selling fish, I spend my spare time walking in the Sligo mountains" says Maura O'Boyle when explaining the enjoyment she takes in her first venture into the world of fish retailing.

"I learned about fish on a Norwegian factory ship. We were supposed to be on the boat four weeks on, four weeks off, but on my first time out I spent three months on board. We sailed around Norway, the Faro Islands and the Western Isles of Scotland."

Maura O'Boyle is a first-generation fish retailer, which is unusual in Ireland. But her passion comes from a love of the sea, and an ability to enjoy the wild and the remote. "When I wake up, if I couldn't see the sea I'd go mad. It gets into your blood."

Nowadays, with fish sourced from all over Ireland, Maura sells from her mobile retail shop. She's in Ballyhaunis on Wednesday, Ballaghaderreen on Thursday and Castlerea on Friday.

Celtic Fish Caterers

Tully, Corcreaghy,
Dundalk,
Co Louth

Tel: 042 9384445

Contact Ian and Antoinette
Lawrence

Open 10am-6pm Mon-Sat

Ian was a fisherman and, according to Antoinette "knows by looking at something whether it's good or not". This has been one of the reasons for the early success of Celtic Fish Caterers, a new venture in the north east.

Celtic Fish Caterers make a good number of frozen products from their small factory just outside Tallinstown. There's haddock in breadcrumbs, calamari, monkfish, prawns in garlic butter, cod cakes and crab cakes. But their real speciality is hand-produced dressed crab, presented properly in the shell with a mixture of delicious seasonings. Needless to say all the locals are delighted with this new enterprise. "All the local farmers come in and they're wanting to try all the new stuff" says a delighted Antoinette. For the word is getting out. The quality of foods cooked and sold by Celtic Fish Caterers would match and improve on that offered by many a restaurant. It's a winning formula.

All the food is cooked in the little factory beside their house. They've converted a third of an acre and there's good parking. They sell to the public straight from the factory, and even though they've only been open for a few weeks at the time of going to press, this operation is already a huge success.

The Fish Cart

55 Laurence St,
Drogheda, Co Louth

Tel: 041 9830622

Contact Patrick Kirwan

Open 8am-6pm Tue-Sat

Peter Kirwan was a fishmonger who sold fish in the centre of Drogheda from a pony and cart, and today his son, Patrick Kirwan, continues this proud family tradition in the centre of Drogheda, selling fish in The Fish Cart - named after his father's cart.

Patrick also started selling fish from a cart in the town, before opening his shop in 1996. Like his father before him, Patrick sources most of his fish from nearby Clogherhead.

During the time the shop has been open, Drogheda has blossomed as a city, with many more people choosing to live in this east coast town. "When we started, we sold on the street and we used to sell for just three days. Now the shop is open for five days a week, and we're busy." Tastes have also changed. "When we first opened we would just sell cod, haddock, whiting and smoked fish, but now people are buying halibut, John Dory, brill, turbot, tuna and swordfish."

The Fish Cart remains a traditional shop to this day, selling fillets of fresh fish, a shop that has stayed true to its roots both in name and in practice.

Morgan's Oceanfresh

Omeath, Co Louth

Tel: 042 9375128
www.morgansoceanfresh.ie

Contact Joe Morgan

Open 10am-6pm Tue-Sat

The Morgan family has been in the fish business for five generations, fishing for salmon and herring since the 1890s and, travelling by horse and cart, 'cadging' their fish in neighbouring counties. Nowadays they concentrate on filleting, distribution, and the development of retail outlets in nearby towns. They also operate a number of fish trailers, and you will find their fresh fish in Navan in Kennedy Rd Car Park, Wed 8am-3pm, Thur-Fri 8am-4pm; Kells, Farrell St, Fri 8am-1pm; Dundalk, Park St, Thur-Fri 8am-3pm, Church St, Fri 8am-3pm & the Newry market on Fri, 8am-1pm. Perhaps the best way to experience Morgan's is to turn up at the factory - not only do they have a thriving shop, but they positively encourage visitors to view traditional fish filleting methods at first hand.

Johnny Morgan's Fish Shop

7 Eimer Court
Dundalk, Co Louth

Tel: 042 9327977

Contact Colm Morgan

Open 9am-5.30pm Tue-Fri,
9am-3pm Sat

Colm Morgan is the fourth, or maybe he's the fifth, generation of his family to sell fish in County Louth. "It goes back as long as anyone can remember", he says simply.

The Morgan forebears began by "fishing for herring in Carlingford Lough - the real horse and cart thing. My grandfather and his father started selling herring in Dundalk. It all started from there."

This progressed to "buying a wee van back in the thirties" when Colm's father got involved. And both father and son started a fish stall in the town, just outside the Ulster Bank.

Today, the shop is in Eimer Court in Dundalk. It's a tiny shop, with a great aesthetic and sense of style. Their policy is, quite simply, the very best for selling fish: "We try to get rid of everything each day, and then start again the next. We strive to re-stock on a daily basis."

Connolly's Seafood

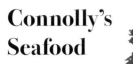

43 Trimgate Street, Navan, County Meath

Tel: 046 9072233

Contact Kieran Connolly

Open 8.30am-5.30pm Tue-Fri, 8.30am-1pm Sat

The Connolly family history in seafood comes from their long experience in fishing, and today the family still all work as fishermen. In 2002 Connolly's Seafood was opened in ever-expanding Navan. It has been hugely successful, and this year they fittted a newly designed counter, built like a wave, to encompass the enormous variety of fish they sell in what is a relatively small space in Trimgate Street.

Their audience are there for them. "People are eating a lot more fish" says Noleen Connolly. "They are more aware of their diets, and there were never as many cookery programmes. More people are cooking at home, and we see the result of it."

Nick'sFish

Town Centre, beside the Post Office, Ashbourne County Meath

Tel: 01-8353555
www.nicksfish.ie
Contact Nicholas Lynch

Open 10am-6pm Mon-Fri, 10am-5pm Sat

Nicholas Lynch's renowned wholesale business opened this flagship shop in 2007. Nick's Fish sells an eclectic selection of fish including the award-winning Loch Duart salmon, and a range of organic wines. One of their specialities, and indeed one of their most popular items, is their epicurian seafood mix. The mix uses premium fish, carefully deboned.

The fishing industry is part of Mr Lynch's heritage. His mother was from Inis Meain in the Aran Islands. "The sea was their only option" he says of his maternal family. "It took a huge toll in those days, my mother lost many relatives to the sea."

Nick's Fish is now a vital addition to Ashbourne, a pristine, superbly run outfit that is worth going out of your way to visit.

Beshoff's the Market

17/18 West Pier,
Howth, Co Dublin

Tel: 01 8397555
Contact Alan Beshoff
www.beshoffs.ie
Open 8am-6pm Mon-Sat, 9am-
6pm Sun

Beshoff's slogan is "It's never just fish".

"It's our passion, our way of life. We're proud to be traditional fishmongers supplying the freshest, best-quality seafood available, naturally and responsibly."

With Beshoff's the Market they've taken this motto a step further. Next to a superbly stocked fish counter you will find fresh organic fruits and vegetables, wines, oils and sauces. There is a coffee bar, oyster bar and a critically-regarded restaurant. They have utensils for the kitchen, flowers for the table. "I want people to be able to come in, have a cup of coffee, buy the *Irish Times*, maybe get some flowers, and some mackerel" says Alan.

Beshoff's is an essentials shop, and everything is ethically sourced, organic or wild, and beautifully presented.

Caviston's

59 Glasthule Road,
Sandycove,
Co Dublin

Tel: 01 2809120

(Restaurant telephone: 01
2809245)

Contact David Caviston

Open 8.30am-6pm Mon-Sat

It may be time to hand out the bus pass and the pension to Caviston's, for this landmark destination firm is just over 60 years old. And yet, Caviston's remains one of the most progressive shops in Dublin.

Today, this Glasthule landmark is staffed by a new generation of the family: Mark, who manages the front deli; David, who is in charge of fish and organic vegetables; and Lorraine who heads up the office.

Caviston's was started three generations ago by grandfather John Caviston, and his brother. It opened as a fish shop with a small counter. This expanded to a fish and vegetable shop, then a few jars of preserves were put on the shelves, then some eggs, and bit by bit it progressed to become one of Dublin's foremost delicatessens. A hugely successful restaurant was added, and now they employ a staff of up to 35 people.

"In the shop we focus on things you can't get in supermarkets. We always ask our suppliers, what do you have that's different?", says David. But every detail of Caviston's is different, and not simply different, but better. It's always been the sort of place where you can actually recall every detail of your first visit. On our first visit, Peter Caviston gave us a verbatim recipe for onion sauce to go with smoked haddock. What's the memory of your first visit?

Doran's on the Pier

7 West Pier, Howth
Co Dublin

Tel: 01 8392419
www.seafood2go.ie

Contact Sean Doran

Open 9am-6pm Mon-Sat,
10am-6pm Sun

If you talk to Sean Doran for any length of time you begin to realise that he is a person whose work embraces the political, the economic, the cultural and the historical spheres, not to forget the culinary culture. He is part owner, with John Aungier, of the Oar House Restaurant, and he has a thriving wholesale fish business. He runs a shop selling fresh fish, and a website home delivery service. He is working in a company that has over 50 years of experience in the seafood business, and he is a consultant to the Seychelles fishing industry, advising them on fishing policy.

The Doran's on the Pier shop is situated on Howth Pier, next to the Oar House Restaurant. Due to be expanded in 2009, it is an excellent fish shop selling a wide range of fish and shellfish. Doran's on the Pier also run a new website - www.seafood2go.ie - which is open to both the trade and the public. You can buy fish for home delivery, and there are many special offers and bargains to be had on the site.

Their website sums up their retail policy effectively: "At Doran's we select only the best and freshest seafood from directly off the local boats, and literally from Malin Head to Mizen Head. And with the changing cultural spectrum and the demands for more exotic types of fish, we fly in twice weekly fish such as sea bream, swordfish, fresh sardines, catfish, tilapia and carp to name but a few. So if you are looking for a traditional cut of cod or long ray, want to have that special dinner with black sole, turbot or monkfish or maybe something more exotic like baked seabass or tuna for the barbecue, Doran's on the Pier is the place to come."

Howth is also the place to go at the weekend, and Doran's opens for the weekend trippers who often call into the shop to buy fish... to give to the seals in the harbour just outside!

Egan's Ocean Fresh

85a Strand Street,
Skerries, Co Dublin

Tel: 01 8495244
www.egansfreshfish.com

Contact Tony Gunnery

Open 9am-6pm Tue-Sat
11am-3pm Mon

Connie Egan and her daughter Bridget and grand-daughter Carmel carried on the business of selling fish for three generations before Tony Gunnery, Carmel's son, took the helm of Egan's Ocean Fresh.

Connie was a great businesswoman with four shops facing the Coombe maternity hospital. Aided by her children, hers was an essential stop for people from the Midlands to take home a bit of fish when the new baby was born, and this demand from inland led the family to try their hand at selling fish in Mullingar.

The story goes that the four boxes of herring sent on the train from Heuston to Mullingar in 1932 sold out in two minutes. So began Egan's market stall in Mullingar, which still exists today, and Egan's are the longest trading business in the town.

Tony also runs a quaint little shop in the lovely area of Strand Street, next to the fishing harbour, in picturesque Skerries. "We're just here to sell fish" says Mr Gunnery, and that's what they do: good-quality flat fish, chunky fillets of turbot, brill and John Dory, plenty of plaice and mackerel.

JL Fitzsimmons Fish Shop

183a Kimmage
Road West,
Crumlin Cross,
Dublin

Tel: 01 4554832
Contact Philip Fitzsimmons

Open 10am-5.30pm Tue-Fri,
10am-4pm Sat

JL Fitzsimmons Fish Shop is something of a Dublin institution. For the last 15 years it has been under the ownership of John Fitzsimmons and these days the shop is run by Philip Fitzsimmons, John's son. It remains a lovely spot to source pristine fish, sold by Philip with helpful charm.

Philip's enjoyment for fish is infectious. "My favourite fish is John Dory. And, once it's fresh, there's not much better than fresh mackerel." But, because of his location, by far the biggest selling fish in this, Dublin's heartland, is ray.

So how do Dubliners cook ray? "Flour it and fry it in a bit of butter, or bake it. Or, if you have time, dip it in a bit of batter and eat it doused in salt and vinegar."

"If we didn't have ray we'd have to shut the place!" says Philip.

Kish Fish

40/42 Bow Street,
Smithfield, Dublin 7
Tel: 01-8543900

Open 9am-4.30pm Tue-Fri,
9am-1pm Sat

Malahide Road Industrial Park,
Coolock, Co Dublin
Tel: 01-8543925

Open 8am-5pm Mon-Fri,
8am-2pm Sat

www.kishfish.ie

Contact Bill, Tadgh, Damian or
Fedelmia O'Meara

Since 1966 Kish Fish has developed purposefully and organically, beginning with Tadgh O'Meara Snr's wholesale business in the Smithfield market, and onwards to a state-of-the-art retail and wholesale business serving two highly respected shops in Dublin.

Brothers Bill, Tadgh and Damian run the business with their mother Fedelmia, and a glance at their website will underline the ambition and intellect behind this impressive operation. The website is worth any seafood lover's time to discover tips on how to recognise fresh fish, understanding seasonality and nutrition, and has some delicious recipes and tips for matching wine with fish.

The acumen displayed in their website is equally evident in their two retail shops. The original Kish is in Smithfield, very near to where many Dubliners will remember the location of the old Dublin fish market. In Coolock they have a large modern premises where the displays are large enough to display whole fish - a great confidence booster for the customer. Both shops are noted for their value and freshness.

Kish Fish - named after the Kish Lighthouse – is a fabulous mix of the traditional – "Our filleters all come from the stock that worked the market" – and the modern. These are community shops that attract visitors from everywhere, and this is a family business that is as professionally run as you can find.

Lett's
Craft Butchers

Main Street, Newcastle,
Co Dublin

Tel: 01 458 0156
www.lettscraftbutchers.com

Contact John Lett
Open 9am-6.30pm Mon-Sat

John Lett opened a fish counter in his excellent butcher's shop "because I wanted to sell everything fresh". So along with award-winning sausages, artfully butchered locally-sourced meat and organic chickens, you can buy the freshest and most professionally prepared seafood fillets. The fish is supplied by Kish Fish, and it matches the superb quality and stylishness that this shop exudes. This is a gem of a shop, a mixture of artisan craftmanship and a sophisticated design ethic.

Nicky's Plaice

Store F, West Pier
Howth, Co Dublin

Tel: 01 8326195
Contact Martin McLoughlin

Open 10am-1pm Mon, 9am-6pm Tue-Fri, 9am-8pm Thur, 9am-4pm Sat

Four generations of the McLoughlin family have played their part in establishing Nicky's Plaice as an iconic destination in Irish fish retailing, and Martin McLoughlin is the perfect person to carry on the tradition.

Nicky's is still a family business, with both brother and brother-in-law, and Nicky McLoughlin Snr, playing their part in the business, and the location of Nicky's Plaice, at the very end of Howth Pier, makes this fish shop the archetypal idea of what a fish shop should look like and what it should offer.

"The location has huge impact. It's unique, you feel you are coming back to the home of fish. The history attached to it is older than any of us, but the expertise and knowledge still stands. We are still working on improving that today," says Mr McLoughlin.

Expect a wide range of very fresh fish, the most popular of which are cod, haddock, ray and plaice. They also smoke their own salmon.This is a proud shop with a real sense of mission. and Martin McLoughlin makes much of his respect for the sea. "Fish is one of the last things that man has gone out to hunt."

Out of the Blue

Unit 28 Millennium
Business Park,
Cappagh Road,
Dublin 11

Tel: 01 8649233

Contact Brian O'Callaghan

Leopardstown Friday market,
Temple Bar & Naas Saturday
market.

The East Coast Inshore Fishing Company act as commission agents for fishing boats, sourcing fresh fish direct from the boats and distributing them to independent fish mongers and shops, and supplying their own renowned market fish stalls in the various city and south city Dublin farmers' markets. Their fish vans trade under the name Out of the Blue, and no visit to the Leopardstown, Temple Bar or Naas farmers' markets should be undertaken without buying fish from these notable sellers. The company East Coast actually dates back to 1942, and has been in the O'Callaghan family since 1971.

Ocean Marine

25a Monkstown Farm,
Monkstown, Co Dublin

Tel: 01 2802842

Contact Darren Rogerson

Open 9am-6pm Tue-Sat

The Rogerson family typify everything you would expect from a family so connected with the sea. George Rogerson began his career fishing in Fleetwood in Liverpool with his father and brothers. His mother, also from a fishing family, came from Dun Laoghaire, which explains why the family settled in South Dublin. George's grandmother had a fish stall in Dun Laoghaire, today run by his auntie Vera. George progressed from selling fish on the pier to the company he started 30 years ago, Ocean Marine. He works now on the site of an old credit union, with his son Darren and wife Lee. Ocean Marine is a processing unit with a retail shop to be opened in April 2009. The sea has claimed many in the family, brothers and uncles. "That's the other side of it", says Lee with resignation. But, as many of the people described in this directory agree, fishing and all that is connected with it is "in the blood".

Ocean Path

West Pier, Howth,
County Dublin

Tel: 01 8398900

Contact Alan Ecock
Open 9am-6pm Tue-Fri

With more than 42 years in the industry, Alan Ecock's Ocean Path are the largest processors of fresh seafood in Ireland, supplying Superquinn, M&S, Supervalu, Centra and Dunnes amongst others with a vast range of fresh seafood, frozen fish and value-added seafood products, and their traditionally smoked salmon, Dunns of Dublin.
   Their shopfront for retailing to the public can be found in Ireland's seafood Mecca, the West Pier at Howth, where you will find a superb range of Irish fish, deep-sea fish, shellfish and exotics. This is nothing less than the oldest fish company in Ireland – established back in 1822, and it is still family-run, an institution dedicated to quality.

Select Seafoods

Units 7-8 Butterly
Business Park,
Kilmore Road, Artane,
Dublin 5

Tel: 01 8486839

Contact Christine Gibney

Open 6am-5pm Tue-Fri,
6am-3pm Sat

"I'm up at five, I'm in here at six and I could be here still at seven in the evening. I'm hands on!", says Christine Gibney of the company she started 16 years go, after 15 years experience in the business. "I started with a car, I didn't even have a van, but today we have three vans, a small factory and a small retail shop." This steady development has allowed Christine to put her seafood expertise into practice for the benefit of the customers of Select Seafoods, and today she still has some of the original clients who first did business with her on day one. "I would say I still have five or six of my original customers, and I have only lost others because their businesses have closed".
   What's the secret of Select Seafoods? "I love it. I always say to my customers, 'If you want or need something, I'm always at the end of a 'phone'".

Stevie Connolly's Seafood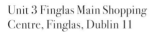

Unit 3 Finglas Main Shopping
Centre, Finglas, Dublin 11

Tel: 01 8568564

Contact Stevie Connolly

Open 8am-6pm Tue-Fri, 8am-
2pm Sat

"Dublin is a great place for fish" says Stevie Connolly. "I get all the locals coming in, and they understand fish. They buy it regularly." Stevie's shop is in the old Dublin village of Finglas, and it's a place that he feels is part of the reason for the success of the shop.

"In working class areas, people always bought fish." It's historical, it's cultural, with its animus often leading back to religious practices, as well as economic factors. "My busiest days are still Wednesday and Friday."

Stevie Connolly's is also a regional shop. "There are certain things, like black sole, that wouldn't sell. I buy for my market, which means smoked fish and white fish fillets and, of course, ray." A lot of the fish is sourced directly from the Connolly family trawlers. "My dad has been fishing for the last forty years and my brother is a fisherman."

The company does a little bit of wholesale in the area, but they concentrate mostly on retail. This is a classic Dublin shop - a real treasure.

Thomas Mulloy

12 Lwr Baggot St,
Dublin 2

Tel: 01 6611222

www.mulloys.ie

Contact Tommy & Ross Mulloy

Open 9am-5.50pm Tue-Fri,
9am-3.50pm Sat

Mulloy's is a long-established, city-centre shop whose specialisation in excellent prime fish and shellfish is matched by an equal expertise in the selling of seasonal game birds. The company is presently expanding, with imminent plans to open a shop along the West Pier in Howth.

Wrights of Marino

21 Marino Mart
Fairview
Dublin 3

Tel: 01 8333636
www.wrightsofmarino.com

Contact Jeff Wright

Open 10.30am-2.30pm Mon,
9am-5pm Tue-Thu, 9am-
5.30pm Fri, 10am-3.30pm Sat

"If it swims - we have it!!" is the famous logo of Wrights of Marino, and this smart piece of sloganeering is no idle boast. Wrights specialise in selling exotic fish. So if you are looking for yellowfin tuna or line caught sea bass, this is the place to start.

As with so many other Irish fishmongers, it has taken generations of patient expertise and dedicated commitment to build Wrights of Marino into the seafood wholesaler that most of Dublin's restaurateurs turn to when sourcing fresh fish. The company started as a small fish shop at the beginning of the last century, and has steadily developed into a business that includes wholesaling, importing and the exporting of seafood in Ireland and throughout the world. They also operate a smokehouse, producing and selling not only smoked salmon but also smoked cod, haddock, coley, mackerel, trout and cured gravadlax.

At the heart of the business, however, is the Wrights of Marino shop, which has been in the same ownership, selling fresh fish to Dubliners, from the same spot, for nearly 100 years.

Atlantis Seafoods

Rosslare Road,
Wexford, Co Wexford

Tel: 053 912 3309

Contact: John Kenny

Open 9am-6pm Mon-Sat

John Kenny's Atlantis has joined forces with Doyle's Country Store, an emporium on Wexford's 1798 Street, selling a bit of fish, a bit of meat, some cakes, vegetables and fruit. Most of the fish comes from nearby Kilmore Quay.

In their factory on the Rosslare Road they also operate their own traditional smoke house, smoking salmon, trout, cod, haddock and mackerel.

There is a steely and precise professionalism at play in the company that run Atlantis, for they also operate a nationwide network of fish wholesaling and, in 2009, Atlantis will be launching an exciting new product range, which, it is hoped, like the distribution arm of Atlantis, will go nationwide.

Skipper's Seafoods

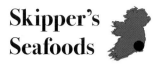

Drinagh, Wexford, Co Wexford

Tel: 053 9142592

Contact BiBi and Jason

Markets: Bagnelstown, Wed 9am-noon; Bunclody, Wed 1pm-4pm; Thurles, Thur 9am-4pm;Tullamore, Thur 9am-4pm, Portlaois, Fri 9am-3pm, Tipperary, Fri 9am-2pm, Carlow, Sat 9am-2pm

Look out for BiBi and Jason's Skipper's Seafoods in country markets throughout the south west. Amongst the many markets they operate in you will find them in Tullamore, Portlaois, Carlow and Bunclody.

Whelan's

Curraghmore
Salt Mills,New Ross,
Wexford, Co Wexford

Tel: 051 562158

Contact Suzie Whelan

Open 9.30am-5.30pm Thur & Fri

You will find Suzie and Patrick Whelan's fish retailing operation at the end of a lane, just off the Wexford new line. Their shop is actually a converted old van with a chill cabinet, and most of their fish comes off their own boat in Kilmore Quay. It's only open two days a week, but Whelan's is one of the best, and most atmospheric places to buy fish in County Wexford.

Casey's Fish Shop

Abercorn Square,
Strabane, Co Tyrone

Tel: 048 7138 2622

Contact Eileen Casey

Open 9am-5.30pm Mon-Sat

Casey's family businesses are comprised of both Casey's salmon, a wholesale fish distribution business distributing both north and south, and Casey's Fish Shop, a small retail shop in Abercorn Square, where fine fish is sold by enthusiastic staff to happy customers. It's a typical Northern Irish fish operation, where the modest scale of the enterprise works effectively and efficiently to guarantee the high quality of the fish that is both sourced intelligently by Eileen, and sold knowledgeably by her staff.

SEAFOOD CIRCLE

*Get to know
who really knows seafood*

For expertise and excellence when shopping
for seafood or dining out, look for the Circle

seafoodcircle.ie

IASC 'SEAFOOD CIRCLE' MEMBERSHIP

The BIM Seafood Circle recognises and supports retail and hospitality businesses that consistently deliver the highest standards of seafood and service to their customers.

Wondering where to buy great quality seafood?
Need help or advice when buying seafood?
BIM "Seafood Specialist" members have the answers.

In recognition of their in-depth knowledge and skills, 26 IASC members are delighted to be acknowledged "Seafood Specialists" under the BIM Seafood Circle initiative. Also, six members have a seafood pub or restaurant as part of their seafood portfolio. The names are:

Seafood Specialist

Beshoff's the Market
Burren Smokehouse
Caviston's
Central Fish Market
Clarke's Seafood
   Delicatessen
Connemara
   Smokehouse

Dorans on the Pier
Fishy Fishy Shop
J&L Fitzsimons
Galway Bay Seafoods
Johnny Morgan's
Kay O'Connell
Kirwan's Fish Cart
Kish Fish

Morgan's Oceanfresh
Nick's Fish
Nicky's Plaice
Rene Cusack
Stevie Connolly
   Seafood
Wrights of Marino
Yawl Bay Seafoods

Hospitality

Caviston's Seafood Restaurant
Fishy Fishy Café
Ivans Oyster Bar & Grill
McDonaghs
Meadowlands Hotel
The Oar House

Get to know who really knows seafood - **www.seafoodcircle.ie**

glossary

Arctic Charr is both a freshwater and saltwater fish, found in deep, cold, glacial lakes. It is now farmed in Ireland by Cloonacool Artic Charr (www.cloonacoolarcticcharr.ie). Artic Char has a similar sweet, earthy delicious taste to that of freshwater trout; it has the same characteristic pinky flesh and delicacy. It is available all year round and suits being filleted, grilled and served with a rich sauce.

Black Sole is the king of all the soles with its dark brown skin and sweet, juicy, close-grained flesh. In the UK it is known as Dover Sole, and many great recipes have been invented just for this fish. Don't buy it in the months January and February, July and August, but otherwise it's a year round treat. Classed as a flat, coldwater fish it is best cooked on the bone, a few days after it has been caught. Alternatives are Lemon Sole and Witch.

Bream is both a saltwater fish – Sea Bream, or a freshwater fish – Fresh Bream. The sea fish has the better flavour, and farmed Gilthead Sea Bream has made this beautiful-looking fish more readily available. A round fish, it is quite bony and needs to be scaled. You can steam it whole, bake it in foil or deep fry it. It has a similar flavour, look and texture to Sea Bass. Black Bream is the most commonly-caught wild species and you might be lucky enough to find this during the months of July to December.

Brill is often compared unfavourably to Turbot, which is unfair, because it has the most beautiful sweet taste that would easily match its big brother in terms of flavour. Small Brill can be cooked on the bone, but the larger fish suit being filleted or cut into tranches and pan-fried. Brill is classified as a flat, coldwater fish, and has a firm, moist, gelatinous texture. Don't eat the skin, because it's bitter.

Clams are molluscs, best eaten in spring and summer. It's hard to find them in fish shops, but go for a walk on the coast off the west of Ireland and you should spot the clam pickers who somehow manage to pursuade these little creatures to give themselves up from the gritty beach in order to be shipped off to Spain. Clams make great soup, and they combine well with other fish in cassseroles. A classic way to prepare them is to cook them in a tomato sauce and serve with spaghetti. They taste of the sea.

Cod has a well-documented history of political significance, and this versatile, round, coldwater fish is one of the most popular fish of any that are caught in these waters. The best way to buy Cod is to buy from a large fish that has been cut into steaks or supremes. It is easy to remove any bones and you have in front of you the evidence of why this is such a popular fish. Alternatives to Cod are Haddock, Coley, Hake and any number of Cod-like species that are fished in these waters. You can cook Cod any way that fish is cooked.

Coley or Saithe is a good, sustainable version of a Cod-like fish. It is similar to Black Pollack and has a clean, buttery taste and flaky texture. When smoked it is almost indistinguishable from smoked Cod. Coley needs to be fresh, and like cod, it is a round, coldwater fish. Try poaching it to bring out the best. Coley is always very good value.

Crab is available from March to September, peaking in quality and availability from May to June. Crab is extremely good for you, so eat it regularly. The most common variety of crab eaten in these waters is brown crab. Female crabs have more brown meat, males are prized by restaurateurs because they have more white meat. Buy them alive and twitching from fish tanks.

Dab is a flat coldwater fish, similar in shape to Halibut and in flavour and texture to Plaice. It's another good value fish because it is isn't well known, and not only is it sustainable, it's good to eat. You will find it in the summer and early autumn and you can use it to grill, fry or bake whole.

Grey Mullet is a popular restaurant fish, because chefs appreciate its good taste and the fact that it is like a cheaper version of Sea Bass. You can also substitute Sea Bream for any recipe that includes Grey Mullet. Mullet has a good, meaty, chewy texture and a sweet nutty flavour that combines well with rich sauces.

Gurnard belongs to a family of quite a number of different species, but the ones we can buy are usually Red Gurnard and Grey Gurnard. Both are superb-flavoured, round, coldwater fish that have a good muscular texture which won't fall apart when cooking. This makes them perfect for casseroles, but Red Gurnard in particular looks spectacular when roasted on the bone. A sustainable fish that you will continue to buy once you've cooked it once.

Haddock is a fish we should eat with caution to help preserve dwindling stocks. It comes from the same family as Cod and Pollack and is distinguished visually by its strong black lateral line. Haddock is *the* best fish for smoking because of its sweet taste and firm texture. It is a round, coldwater fish that is usually sold filleted. Good pan-fried and superb for using in fish pies or fishcakes, Haddock is also unbeatable when battered and served with chips.

Hake is beginning to be valued here as much as it is in Spain for its ability to match up to the much-loved Mediterranean flavours of garlic, herbs and tomatoes. This is definitely a prime fish with a fantastic taste and a melting, open texture.

Halibut is the largest flat fish in the ocean, and, when you can find it, it has a dense, satisfying, sticky, flaky texture and a surprisingly subtle rooty flavour. Part of the Halibut's favourite diet are the eggs of sea birds, which must go some way to explain its deliciousness. Unfortunately, restaurants hoover up most of the halibut that hits the market and it's hard to find. Buy it when you see it.

Herring is almost never sold in fish shops, because most of it is processed into either Swedish marinated Herring, roll mops or kippers. But if you can find this oil-rich, round, coldwater cousin to mackerel, then eat it fresh and grill it or bake it whole. The Herring comes from the same family as Sprats or Pilchards.

John Dory or St Peter's fish, named because of its characteristic thumb mark, actually comes from the French name jaune doré, which means 'golden yellow'. Like Monkfish, the large-eyed head of a John Dory accounts for no less than half of its weight. This means a low yield; only 35% of John Dory is edible. It's a unique species, not related to either flat or round fish, but what little you get from it is certainly worth having. The flavour is robust and the skin crunchy. It pairs beautifully with strong acidic partners, salsas and Mediterranean flavours.

Lemon Sole may be regarded as the poor cousin to Black Sole, but this lovely oval-bodied fish has its many devotees. Cook it the same way as you would cook Black Sole – on the bone with rich buttery sauces. Alternatives are other flat, coldwater fish such as Plaice and Witch, which share the same gentle balance of acidity and shortbread-like sweetness.

Ling is a fish from the same family as Cod, Pollack or Haddock. It's a slow-growing, round, coldwater fish with a dense texture that makes it good in soups and stews. In Ireland Ling is often salted and dried. To cook salted Ling, soak it in water, pan-fry it or poach it in milk, and serve with mashed potatoes.

Lobsters live a solitary life, coming out only at night, when fishermen catch them in pots which have been strategically placed near rocks on the sea bed. They are territorial creatures, defending their space with their fearsome claws. Many people are nervous about cooking lobster at home, especially as you have to buy these heavily-armed creatures alive. But once you've done it once, you'll learn and gain in confidence. The RSPCA recommend that you put live lobsters in the freezer for two hours before cooking, after which they will become unconscious. Thereafter a sharp knife, thrust into the top of the head results in instantaneous death, and stops the flesh from becoming tense and tough. Everything about the lobster is so precious, from the fact that you yourself kill have to kill it, to its spectacular taste. So keep it simple and serve with just a little butter.

Mackerel is one of the richest sources of precious and necessary Omega 3 oils, which is one reason why it's become so popular. Another reason is its taste. Closely related to the Tuna family, this is one of the best fishes not only to catch yourself, but to cook. In the summer you need to cook mackerel on the day it's caught. The North Sea mackerel we get in the winter has more fat, and lasts a little longer. Mackerel is characteristically mixed with acidic flavours which counteract its oiliness. So don't be surprised to see it paired with such unlikely ingredients as rhubarb, gooseberry or orange. If you know how fresh it is, and it's got to be fresh, then eat it raw with some wasabi and soy sauce, Japanese-style.

Monkfish are certainly the ugliest fish in the sea. They are not related in any way to the other flat or round fish we catch in these waters, so they are not only ugly but uniquely ugly. There are similar fish found on the other side of the world (they're known as 'stargazers'), but these don't have monk's all-important characteristic and best feature: its tail. For while the head occupies fifty percent of the fish, that tail, with its lobster-like taste and chicken-like texture is the important bit. Roast it, grill it, fry it, wrap it in bacon. Just don't overcook it, or it will dry out.

Mussels found in most fish shops are either dredged or rope grown. Rope grown are best because they don't pick up grit, and because they are always covered with water they keep on feeding and growing fat. Buy mussels from a fishmonger; don't be tempted to pick them off a rock. A mussel needs to be purified, otherwise you run the serious risk of eating some E. coli along with your shellfish. Also, make sure to 'beard' them, which means pulling the little tuft away from the centre of the mussel.

Oysters are molluscs that are either Native Oysters, or Pacific (or Rock) Oysters. The former are only eaten in the months with an 'r' in, and are best eaten raw, because it would be a shame to cook out that incredible steely flavour. Pacific oysters are delicious too, meatier and plumper than the Native, but not as clean tasting. Use Pacific for any cooked Oyster recipe. Pacific oysters are available all year round.

Plaice is a flat coldwater fish that tastes better towards the end of the year (don't eat it between February and April because it is 'in roe' at this time, and the flesh becomes thin and watery). It should be eaten as fresh as possible, and you can tell instantly whether or not it's fresh by the orange dots that are scattered on its skin. These will fade quickly in time, so if they're not bright orange, don't buy that fish. One of the most distinctive things about Plaice is its smell, which just about anybody who eats fish will be able to conjure up in a moment of thought. When everything comes right for this fish, its freshness, the right season, the right size, then it's king of the sea. Bake it whole if it's a large fish, pan fry small fish fillets.

Pollack is a family of two species, White Pollack, which is the sought-after one, and Black Pollack which is very similar to Coley. Part of the Cod family, Pollack suits all types of cooking and is just as versatile as its Cod-cousin. You can tell when a fish is getting popular, because you begin to see it on restaurant menus. Such is true with White Pollack, which is now prized for its nutty flavour, versatile nature, and succulent texture.

Prawns in this country mean the Dublin Bay Prawn, or Langoustine. This is the best of all the shellfish that come under the umbrella of the prawn family, and the fact that you eat only a fraction of the fish doesn't take away from its popularity (those bones can always go to make a great stock or sauce after all). Buy prawns that are alive and still twitching, eat the tail and cook quickly so they don't turn mushy.

Ray (Skate) is the fish that is most closely associated with Dublin (Ringsend, by the sea in inner Dublin, used to be known as Raytown). But the customers of Fishy Fishy Cafe are getting quite a taste for it too! Martin serves it off the bone, and it's one of the most popular things on the menu. Certainly you must get your fishmonger to skin it, and if you can get it boned it's quite delicious, due to its extraordinarily meaty texture. Classically it's served with browned butter and capers, but try it in fish cakes too. Like Shark, Ray is a cartilaginous fish, which means it actually doesn't have bones at all. In fact Ray is closely related to Shark, and, for those who care about these things, it's the pectoral fins that you eat, not its 'wings'. A word of warning, it simply *must* be fresh, otherwise it tastes of ammonia. Sadly, many species of Skate are on the critical list of endangered species.

Red Mullet is a deep-sea fish that is usually served on the bone. It's a round, warmwater species that suits Mediterranean flavours. Eating this fish needs to be a totally chilled-out experience to get the most from it, so try roasting it and eating it straight from the roasting dish, pulling the flesh away with your fingers.

Salmon is no longer available in its wild form. We can only buy farmed, so just make sure you are buying from a reputable source. The up-side of this is that good-quality salmon is now once again available and sold at a good price. Salmon farming on the West Coast of Ireland and the West Coast of Scotland provide good fish, due to the strong currents that keep the fish healthy. Children often get a taste for fish after enjoying salmon.

Scallops are the connoisseur's choice, rewarding those who love to cook with a dense, melting texture and a mellow iodine flavour. Order the shells in advance if you want to use them, and given that you are an official connoisseur, experiment with pairings such as black pudding, avocado or Chinese flavours.

Sea Bass is now successfully farmed, which makes this superb catch much more readily available. You've got to respect its wild predator, spiny-finned brother, however, beloved of anglers who catch them in the surf. The good news is that even though it has a slightly higher fat content, farmed Sea Bass has the same intensity of flavour and because it is so juicy, is easy to cook. Try stuffing and baking it. You can use Gilthead Bream as an alternative.

Sea Trout was always caught as a by-catch of wild Salmon. But now that Salmon is no longer fished in the wild, Sea Trout is becoming very, very scarce. So we have to content ourselves with farmed Sea Trout, which isn't so much of a hardship, because farmed Sea Trout can be very tasty. This is another oil-rich fish, which is exactly the same as brown trout, but it migrates to the sea. It has a chewy greenness to it that speaks of spring. Serve with new potatoes. Its cousin Rainbow Trout, or River Trout, is a freshwater fish, extensively farmed, that makes the much-loved smoked trout fillets.

Squid is a cephalopod that you either love or you hate. And if you love it, you probably have a favourite way of cooking it, which might be long-cooked in stews, or briefly grilled over flame. Either way, you need to cook it quickly or stew it slowly – anything in between and it will be tough. Large squid should always be scored on the inside of the pouch to ensure even cooking. Incidentally, its black ink is a defence mechanism to warn away enemies. Useful.

Swordfish makes its way into Irish waters during the height of the summer. This is the ultimate barbie fish (barbie as in barbecue, not Barbie and Ken, this is a butch meaty fish that holds its own in the heat.) Simply marinate it, and cook it quickly so it doesn't dry out. The bad news, however, is that Swordfish is now a threatened species, so we are advised not to buy it until stocks replenish.

Tuna is the world's favourite fish. So much so that Blue Fin Tuna has been almost fished out of existence. The Tuna we buy in Ireland, whether imported, or, briefly, from Irish summer waters, is usually Yellow Fin or Skipjack (if you ever see Blue Fin Tuna - don't buy it and give a lecture to the person selling it). The best quality is line- or troll-caught Tuna. Don't eat it raw unless you know just about everything about it, its family history, and who is selling it: Sashimi-standard Tuna is an art and a science, and badly handled raw Tuna can make you sick. Given all those warnings, the only other thing you need to remember about Tuna is not to overcook it, for it can become as dry as toast.

Turbot benefits from firm white flesh, a fantastic flavour and a forgiving nature when it's cooked. It's flesh is moist enough to withstand almost anything. Because of this it's one of the prime fishes that suits all types of cooking. Never throw away gelatinous Turbot bones until you have used them to make stock.

Whiting is known as chicken of the sea, probably because of its mellow, dare we say bland, flavour. Pair this fish with flavoursome ingredients like chorizo, chilli or mushrooms. Once you have removed the pin bones, it's a good fish to start to teach children about the joys of eating fish.

Witch is another name for White Sole. It's a flat, coldwater fish that you can use where you would use Lemon Sole or Plaice. It's best cooked on the bone.

glossary

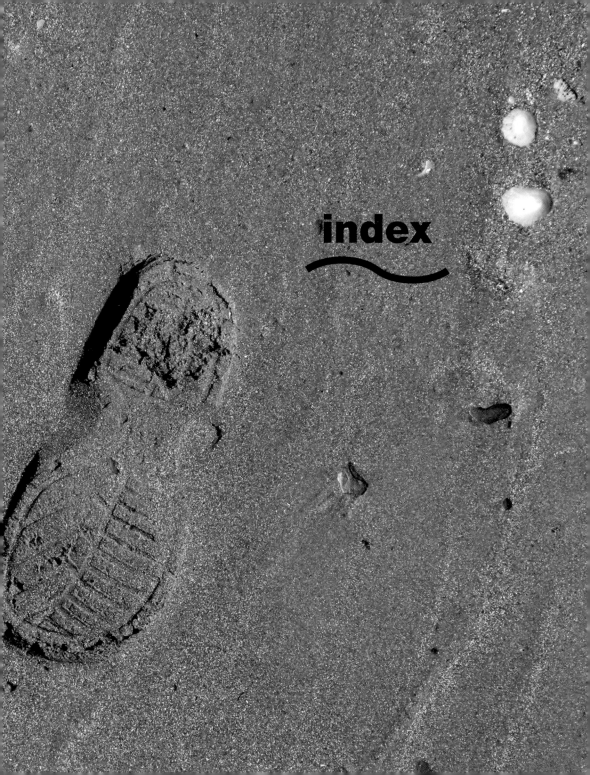

index

W

Y

T